PRAYERS BY THE LAKE
by St. Nikolai Velimirovich

Translated and Annotated by: Rt. Rev. Archimandrite Todor
Mika, S.T.M. and Very Rev. Dr. Stevan Scott

Copyright © 2018
All rights reserve

Contents

INTRODUCTION 8
I 13
II 14
III 16
IV 17
V 18
VI 20
VII 21
VIII 23
IX 25
X 26

XI 28
XII 30
XIII 32
XIV 33
XV 35
XVI 37
XVII 39
XVIII 41
XIX 43

XX	45
XXI	47
XXII	50
XXIII	52
XXIV	53
XXV	54
XXVI	57
XXVII	59
XXVIII	61
XXIX	63
XXX	65
XXXI	67
XXXII	69
XXXIII	71
XXXIV	74
XXXV	76
XXXVI	78
XXXVII	80
XXXVIII	82
XXXIX	84
XL	86

XLI	88
XLII	91
XLIII	93
XLIV	95
XLV	97
XLVI	100
XLVII	103
XLVIII	105
XLIX	108
L	110
LI	113
LII	115
LIII	118
LIV	120
LV	123
LVI	126
LVII	128
LVIII	131
LIX	133
LX	136

LXI	138
LXII	141
LXIII	144
LXIV	146
LXV	148
LXVI	150
LXVII	153
LXVIII	155
LXIX	157
LXX	160
LXXI	162
LXXII	164
LXXIII	166
LXXIV	168
LXXV	171
LXXVI	174
LXXVII	176
LXXVIII	179
LXXIX	181
LXXX	184
LXXXI	187

LXXXII	190
LXXXIII	192
LXXXIV	196
LXXXV	199
LXXXVI	202
LXXXVII	205
LXXXVIII	208
LXXXIX	211
XC	214
XCI	216
XCII	219
XCIII	222
XCIV	224
XCV	227
XCVI	230
XCVII	233
XCVIII	236
XCIX	239
C	242
GLOSSARY	245
Translators Notes to the Introduction	251

St. Nikolai Velimirovich (1881-1956)

INTRODUCTION

Immured by the flesh and blood of a nation, the soul or our people has for centuries been stuttering and struggling as she searched for a tongue to express her pains, her sorrows, her aspirations and her prayers. And she has found her tongue, she has found it in Bishop Nikolai. Through him our stuttering soul has transformed herself into sobbing, such as our eye has never seen, into eloquent prayers, such as our ear has never heard. He is the God-sent fiery tongue, which stands over our soul, and she fervently and passionately confesses to "the Triradiate Master of worlds." He is the style, the grace-filled sumptuous style of our soul. He speaks - as no one among us has ever spoken. He prays — more eloquently than anyone among us has ever prayed. He has the gift of words, for he has the gift of total feeling, the gift of compassion, the gift of total love, the gift of prayer. Up until the time that he appeared — we were desperate: our soul's yearning for Christ was becoming numb, was withering, and was beginning to die. From the moment he appeared - we trembled with joy: our soul's yearning for Christ came back to life in him, it was resurrected and rejuvenated. Rastko's fervent yearning for Christ has taken up its abode in him and has blazed up into a colossal conflagration: and he bums in this conflagration, he burns as a sacrificial holocaust for all mankind. Therefore he has become our optimism, our optimism in the dark days of our own desperate present. We are witnessing a great and rare miracle, a wondrous and holy sign of the times: the blessed Eternity of the Holy Trinity cast anchor the first time on Rastko, and from the Christ-craving Rastko It created the Christ-bearing Sava; that same Eternity has cast anchor a second time, onto Bishop Nikolai, and from the Christ-craving Nikolai It is creating before our eyes the Christ-bearing Nikolai.

These favorites of Eternity know the mystery of our Orthodox soul, they know how the rebellious and Christ-fighting Slavic soul can be molded into a Christlike soul. From Saint Sava up to the present day our Orthodoxy has not had a more eloquent and powerful confessor than Bishop Nikolai. Our optimistic descendants will be captivated with a prayerful awe of him, just as we are in awe of Saint Sava. Our descendants will marvel, and will lament that they will never see what we are seeing with our own eyes, and will never hear what we are hearing with our own ears. For them, as also for many of us, he will be: the hearth where those who have been frostbitten by scepticism and lack of faith will come to thaw and warm themselves.

I read and reread *Prayers by the Lake,* but all their sweet allurement swims into my soul only when I read and reread them *prayerfully.* He, a wonderworker of prayerful rhythms, has power over my soul. I tell myself: "I am locked in the senses, I think by means of the senses, but when his wonderworking prayer flows through my repentant soul, at once the senses, these shackles of the soul, are unshackled, and my soul, my wounded bird, regains her wings and flies off, diving into the sweet depths of Eternity." And my paralyzed heart tells me: "He breaks out of the cocoon of time and space, which engulfs and suffocates your soul, and he drives the butterfly of your soul out into the blue expanses of infinite Eternity." In truth, he is the channel by which Eternity comes forth into my soul and by which my soul enters into Eternity. He strengthens my feeling of personal immortality along with personal eternity, and I feel like a stranger in the world, but like a master of a mansion in Eternity.

He thinks through *prayer,* he philosophizes through prayer. One senses that the luminous souls of the great Orthodox ascetics, especially the mystical soul of St. Simeon the New Theologian, are speaking through him. *Through prayer* he senses God, and through prayer he senses all creation. He is in a prayerful relationship with everything. Orthodoxy, and only Orthodoxy, leads to this. The whole soul collects itself into prayer, for prayer is the only sharp-eyed guide of the mind, the heart and the will.

He speaks about Christ because *he lives by means of Him.* He expands his mysterious lknjkjkbpersonality to divine-human proportions; he experiences a personal, empirical divine incarnation and birth of Christ in his soul. This is reminiscent of the grace-filled empirical Christology of Saint Macarius the Great. Man's purpose is: to give birth to Christ within oneself, to become God, for it is for this reason that God became nourishment for men.

When he turns his soul, moved by prayer, toward creation, he seethes with sadness and starts sobbing with stirring cries. For all creation is sick, wounded, and melancholy. Truly, in his tears "the sadness of all creatures seethes." Truly, in his weeping all human eyes and all human hearts weep. He is afflicted with the pains of all creation; he grieves with the laments of all creatures. Lo, God has sent us a Job who has suffered the sufferings of all mankind and all creation. And yet he is also our Isaiah, who clairvoyantly and inspiringly contemplates suffering in general, and vindicates divine-human suffering in particular.

This world is a sick man, whom sin has made sick, for sin is a sickness, and to scorn sinners is to scorn the sick. With prayer our healer walks around the grievously sick patient, with prayer he walks and with prayer he heals and makes whole. Do not scorn sinners, but pray for them. Feel pity and
compassion for every creature, but do not condemn. Expand and deepen your soul with prayer, and you will begin to cry over the mystery of the world bitterly and vehemently. Make your heart prayerful, together with your soul and your mind, and they will become inexhaustible fountainheads of tears for all mankind. The most reverend man of prayer has made his whole soul prayerful, together with his spirit and mind: and he feels the sins of all sinners as though they were his own, and he repents for all sins as though they were his own, as he weeps and sighs.

Prayer expands the boundaries of man to [those of] the Ultimate Man; it makes one sensitive to all pains and sins; it enables one to cry with the eye of all the tearstained and to mourn with the sorrow of all who mourn. Through the wondrous prayers of our psalmist flows the soul of the Ultimate Man. The boundaries of time and space vanish; the prayers have the fragrance of a universal soul: it is not man, the slave of time and space, who speaks, but the Ultimate Man.

Though his Christ-craving soul we have fallen in love with Christ, and while the slaves of time and space slaughter one another over the frail wealth of the earth, our fearless fighter for Eternity stands on the deserted watchtower of our soul. There he kneels, prostrates himself, sobbing and praying for all mankind.

O Lord, who lovest mankind, make me prayerful with the prayerfulness of the Most Reverend Bishop Nikolai.

Father Justin (Popovich) (1922)

I

Who is that staring at me through all the stars in heaven and all the creatures on earth?

Cover your eyes, stars and creatures; do not look upon my nakedness. Shame torments me enough through my own eyes.

What is there for you to see? A tree of life that has been reduced to a thorn on the road, that pricks both itself and others. What else-except a heavenly flame immersed in mud, a flame that neither gives light nor goes out?

Plowmen, it is not your plowing that matters but the Lord who watches.

Singers, it is not your singing that matters but the Lord who listens.

Sleepers, it is not your sleeping that matters but the Lord who wakens.

It is not the pools of water in the rocks around the lake that matter but the lake itself.

What is all human time but a wave that moistens the burning sand on the shore, and then regrets that it left the lake, because it has dried up?

O stars and creatures, do not look at me with your eyes but at the Lord. He alone sees. Look at Him and you will see yourselves in your homeland.

What do you see when you look at me? A picture of your exile? A mirror of your fleeting transitoriness?

O Lord, my beautiful veil, embroidered with golden seraphim, drape over my face like a veil over the face of a widow, and collect my tears, in which the sorrow of all Your creatures seethes.

O Lord, my beauty, come and visit me, lest I be ashamed of my nakedness—lest the many thirsty glances that are falling upon me return home thirsty.

II

Who put me in this bed of worms? Who buried me in the dust, to become a neighbor of snakes and a banquet for worms?

Who pushed me off the high mountain, to become a companion of bloodthirsty and godless men?

My sin and Your justice, O Lord. My sin stretches from the creation of the world, and it is swifter than Your justice.

I count my sins throughout my entire life, throughout the life of my father and all the way back to the beginning of the world, and I say: Truly, the name of the Lord's justice is mercy.

I bear the wounds of my fathers on myself-wounds that I myself was preparing while I was still in my fathers—and now they have all appeared on my soul, like a spotted hide on a giraffe, like a cloak of vicious scorpions that sting me.

Have mercy on me, O Lord, open the floodgate of the heavenly river of Your grace, and cleanse me of leprous evil, so that without this leprosy I may dare to proclaim Your name before the other lepers without them ridiculing me.
At least raise me up by a head above the rotten stench of this bed of worms, to inhale the incense of heaven and return to life.

At least raise me up as high as a palm tree so I can laugh at the serpents chasing my heels.

O Lord, if there has been even one good deed in the course of my earthly journey, for the sake of that one deed deliver me from the companionship of bloodthirsty and godless men.

O Lord, my hope in despair.

O Lord, my strength in weakness.

O Lord, my light in darkness.

Place just one finger on my forehead and I shall be raised. Or, if I am too unclean for Your finger, let a single ray of light from Your kingdom shine upon me and raise me-raise me, from this bed of worms, O my beloved Lord.

III

Are there days gone by, O man, to which you would wish to return? They all attracted you like silk, and now remain behind you like a cobweb. Like honey they greeted you, like stench you bade them farewell. All were totally filled with illusion and sin.

See how all the pools of water in the moonlight resemble mirrors; and how all the days that were lit up with your levity resemble mirrors. But as you stepped from one day to the next, the false mirrors cracked like thin ice, and you waded through the water and mud.

Can a day that has a morning and an evening as doorways be a day?

O luminous Lord, my soul is burdened with illusions and longs for one day—for the day without doorways, the day from which my soul has departed and sunk into the shifting shadows—for Your day, which I used to call my day, when I was one with You.

Is there any happiness gone by, O man, to which you would wish to return?

Of two morsels of the same sweetness the second is the more trite. You would turn your head away in boredom from yesterday's happiness, if it were set out on today's table.

Moments of happiness are given to you only in order to leave you longing for tme happiness in the bosom of the everhappy Lord; and ages of unhappiness are given to you, to waken you out of the drowsy dream of illusions.

O Lord, Lord, my only happiness, will You provide shelter for Your injured pilgrim?

O Lord, my ageless youth, my eyes shall bathe in You and shine more radiantly than the sun.

You carefully collect the tears of the righteous, and with them You rejuvenate worlds.

IV

My elders taught me, when I was a youth, to cling to heaven and earth, lest I stumble. For a long time I remained a child, and for a long time I used to lean on the crutch that they gave me.

But once eternity flooded through me and I felt like a stranger in the world, heaven and earth snapped in two in my hands like a frail reed.

O Lord, my strength, how frail are heaven and earth! They look like palaces built of lead, but they evaporate like water in the palm of the hand in Your presence. Only by their bristling do they conceal their frailty, and frighten uneducated children.

Get out of my sight, suns and stars. Sunder yourselves from the earth. Do not entice me, women and friends. What help can I receive from you, who are helplessly growing old and sinking into the grave?

All your gifts are an apple with a worm in its core. All your potions have passed through someone's entrails many times. Your garments are a cobweb that my nakedness mocks. Your smiles are a proclamation of sorrow, in which your feebleness is screaming to mine for help.

O Lord, my strength, how feeble heaven and earth are! And all the evil that men do under heaven is an admission of feebleness and—infirmity.

Only someone strong dares to do good. Only someone who is nourished and watered with You, my strength, is filled with strength for goodness.

Only someone who sleeps in Your heart knows rest. Only someone who plows before Your feet will enjoy the fruit of his labors.

My childhood, nourished with fear and ignorance, came to an end; and my hope in heaven and earth vanished. Now I only gaze at You and cling to Your gaze in return, O my cradle and my resurrection.

V

Just a little longer and my journey will end. Keep me on the steep path to You just a little longer, O Conqueror of death; because the higher I climb towards You, the more people try to drag me down—into their abyss. The fuller their abyss becomes, the greater their hope is of defeating You. In truth, the fuller the abyss becomes, the further away from the abyss You are.

How stupid the servants of the tree of knowledge are! They do not measure their strength in You, but in their numbers. They do not adopt a law of justice in Your name, but by their numbers. Whichever way the majority of them choose is the way of truth and justice. The tree of knowledge has become the tree of crime, stupidity, and icy darkness.

Truly, the knowledgeable men of this world know everything except that they are servants of Satan. When the last day dawns, Satan will rejoice in the number of people in his harvest. All the meager ears of grain! But in his stupidity, even Satan counts on quantity rather than quality. One of Your ears of grain will be worth more than the entire harvest of Satan. For You, O Conqueror of death, rely on the fullness of the bread of life, and not on numbers.

In vain I tell the godless: "Head for the Tree of Life and you will know more than you could possibly wish to know. From the tree of knowledge Satan fashions a ladder for you to descend into the nether world."

The godless ridicule me and say: "Through the Tree of Life you want to convert us to your God, whom we do not see."

In truth, you will never see Him. The Light that even blinds the eyes of the seraphim will bum your pupils forever.

Of all that thrives in the putrescence of the earth, those who believe in God are the rarest. O lake and mountain, help me to be glad that I, too, am journeying with these most rare, most unlearned, and most despised believers.

Just a little longer, brethren, and our journey will end.

Sustain us just a little longer, O Conqueror of death.

VI

Onto your knees, generations and nations, before the majesty of God! You are quick to fall down on your knees before your bandit leaders, yet you hesitate to fall down on them before the feet of the Almighty!

You say: "Will the Lord really punish us who are so small? If He had made us bigger and stronger, then He would punish us. But as it is, take a look—we are scarcely any taller than a thorn bush along the road compared to the roaring universe around us, yet do you threaten us with punishment by One who is incomparably greater than we are?"

Fools! When your bandit leaders summon you to evil that even causes the universe to tremble, you still say that you are too small. You excuse yourselves by reason of smallness or weakness only when it comes to performing illustrious deeds.

Even if you are small in your own eyes, you are recorded in the book of fate under a great name. Your forefather Adam used to have the greatness of an archangel and used to glisten with an angelic countenance. Therefore, either the reward of an archangel or the punishment of an archangel is designated for you.

When the desire of your forefather creeps into your heart without a sound, the desire to know creation without the Creator, his archangelic countenance darkens like the earth, and his greatness crumbles into trifles—into you, his seed. For he wishes to know trifles and to crumble into trifles, so that he might enter into the trifles, taste them, and test them.

All trifles, all trivial trivia, most come together and turn their face from the earth to the Creator, so that your archangelic forefather may be established once again and so that his face may shine once again with the radiance of a mirror turned toward the sun.

, establish man as You first created him. This sort of man is not Your work. This sort of man created himself. His name is disease—how was there ever disease in Your hands? His name is fear—how could fear have ever come from the Fearless One? His name is malevolence —how could malevolence ever have come from the Benevolent One?

Fill me with Yourself, O my health; fill me with your eternal matinal light, and make disease, fear, and malevolence evaporate out of me-even as a marsh evaporates in the presence of the sun and is transformed into a fertile field!

VII

Would that I could make musicians out of stone, and dancers out of the sand of the lake, and minstrels out of the leaves of all the trees in the mountains, so that they might help me glorify the Lord-and so that the voice of the earth might be heard amidst the choirs of angels!

The sons of men gorge themselves at the table of the absent Master, and do not sing for anyone except themselves and their mouthfuls, which must eventually return to the earth.

Exceedingly sad is the blindness of the sons of men, who do not see the power and glory of the Lord. A bird lives in the forest, and does not see the forest. A fish swims in the water, and does not see the water. A mole lives in the earth, and does not see the earth. In truth, the similarity of man to birds, fish, and moles is exceedingly sad.

People, like animals, do not pay attention to what exists in excessive abundance, but only open their eyes before what is rare or exceptional.

There is too much of You, O Lord, my breath, therefore people do not see You. You are too obvious, O Lord, my sighing, therefore the attention of people is diverted from You and directed toward polar bears, toward rarities in the distance.

You serve Your servants too much, my sweet faithfulness, therefore You are subjected to scorn. You rise to kindle the sun over the lake too early, therefore sleepyheads cannot bear You. You are too zealous in lighting the vigil lamps in the firmament at night, my unsurpassed zeal, and the lazy heart of people talks more about an indolent servant than about zeal.

O my love, would that I could motivate all the inhabitants of the earth, water, and air to hum a hymn to You! Would that I could remove leprosy from the face of the earth and turn this wanton world back into the sort of virgin that You created!

Truly, my God, You are just as great with or without the world.

You are equally great whether the world glorifies You or whether the world blasphemes You. But when the world blasphemes You, You seem even greater in the eyes of Your saints.

VIII

Worlds swarm around You, like bees around a cherry tree in blossom. One world pushes the other aside; one contests the patrimony of the other; one looks upon the other as an intruder in his home. All claim a greater right to You than You Yourself do.

From the effusion of Your fullness swarms are nourished, O inexhaustible Sweetness. All overeat, and all go away hungry.

Of all the swarms the human swarm leaves the most hungry. Not because You did not have food for men, O Master, but because they fail to recognize their nourishment, and so they contend with caterpillars for the same foliage.

Before all creatures, and before all time and sorrow. You, O Lord, formed man in Your heart. You conceived of man first, even though You manifested him last in the rosaries of creation—even as a gardener thinks about the blooming of a rose all the time he is digging and planting the dry rose stems -even as a builder experiences the joy of the domes while planning a church, even though he builds them last.

You gave birth to man in Your heart, before You began creating.
Help my mortal tongue to name this man, this radiance of Your glory, this song of Your blessedness. Should I call him the Ultimate Man? For just as He was contained in Your heart, so also was all the manifested world, including man and the heralds of man, contained in His mind.

And no one knows the Father except the Son, nor does anyone know the Son except the Father.[1] You were like nirvana," O Lord, until the Son was conceived within You, You were without number or name.

How shall I magnify You in the midst of a swarm of hungry caterpillars, which one wind blows onto the blossoming cherry tree and another blows off, and whose entire lifetime is spent between two winds?

O Lord, my dream day and night, help me to magnify You, so that nothing may become great in my heart except You.

Let all creatures magnify You, O Lord, lest they make themselves great instead of You.

Truly, You are exceedingly great, O Lord, would that all our hymns could make You greater!

Even when all the swarms of insects are blown off the blossoming cherry tree, the cherry tree remains the same in its majesty and vernal beauty.

IX

O *Lord, my soul's most cherished mystery,* how light this world is, when I weigh it on a scale with You[1]!

On one side of the scale is a lake of molten gold, and on the other a cloud of smoke.

All my cares, along with my body and its foolish convulsions of sweetness and bitterness-what are they except smoke, beneath which my soul is swimming in a golden lake?

How can I confess to people the mystery that I see through the rings of Your archangels? How can I tell particles about totality? How can fingernails understand the circulation of blood in the body? It is truly painful for one struck dumb with wonder to speak to those deafened by noise.

First comes begetting and then creating. Just as a miraculous thought is quietly and mysteriously begotten in a man, and the begotten thought thereafter creates, so also did the Ultimate Man, the Only-Begotten, appear in You, and thereafter created everything that God can create.

In Your inviolate chastity, through the activity of the All-Holy Spirit, the Son was begotten. This is the begetting of God from above.

---

[1] "You are My son, today I have begotten You" (Ps.2:7). Cf. Heb. 1:5 and 5:5.

As above, so below—the ancients used to say. What happened in heaven happened also on earth. What happened in eternity happened also in time.

You are dear to me, my love, because You are a mystery to me. Every love burns without burning out as long as the mystery lasts. Mystery revealed is love burned out. I promise myself to You with eternal love even as You pledge Yourself to me with eternal mystery.

You have clothed Yourself with seven heavens; You have hidden Yourself too deep for any eyes. If all the suns were to merge into a single eye, they would be unable to burn through all Your veils. You have not concealed Yourself intentionally, O Great Lord, but because of our imperfection. A divided and dissected creature does not see You. You are unhidden only to one who has become one with You. You are unhidden only to one for whom the wall between "I" and "You" has been razed.

O Lord, my soul's most cherished mystery, how light this world is, when I weigh it on a scale with You!

On one side of the scale is a lake of molten gold, and on the other a cloud of smoke.

X

To a silent tongue and a contemplative mind You draw near, O All-Holy Spirit, bridegroom of my soul. You avoid a talkative tongue as a swan avoids a stormy lake. Like a swan you swim across the quiet of my heart and make it fruitful.

Desist from your wordly wisdom, my neighbors. Wisdom is begotten, not made. As Wisdom is begotten in God, so is it begotten on earth. Begotten wisdom creates, but is not created.

So, you braggarts brag about your intellect! What is your intellect except remembering many facts? And if you remember so much, how could you have forgotten the moments of the wondrous begetting of wisdom within you? Sometimes I hear you talking about great thoughts that were born to you unexpectedly without any effort. Who bore these thoughts to you, intellectuals? How were they begotten without a father, if you admit that you did not father them?

Truly I say to you: the father of these thoughts is the All-Holy Spirit, and their mother survives as the virgin corner of your soul, where the All-Holy Spirit still dares to enter.

Thus every wisdom in heaven and on earth is begotten of the Virgin and the All-Holy Spirit. The All-Holy Spirit hovered over the chastity of the first hypostasis, and the Ultimate Man, the Wisdom of God, was begotten.
What the chastity of the Father is in heaven, the virginity of the Mother is on earth. What the action of the Holy Spirit is in heaven, His action is on earth. What the begetting of wisdom is in heaven, the begetting of wisdom is on earth.

O my soul, my eternal surprise! What happened once in heaven and once on earth must happen to you. You must become a virgin, so that you can conceive the Wisdom of God. You must be a virgin, so that the Spirit of God may fall in love with you. All the miracles in heaven and on earth originate from the Virgin and the Spirit.

A virgin gives birth to creative wisdom. A wanton woman creates barren knowledge. Only a virgin can see truth, while a wanton woman can only recognize things. O triune Lord, cleanse the vision of my soul, and bow down Your face over her, so that my soul may glisten with the glory of her Lord, so that the wondrous history of heaven and earth may be unsealed in her, so that she may be filled with glittering like my lake, when the sun hovers above it at noon.

XI

Once I bound myself to You, my love, all other bonds broke.

I see a swallow distraught over its demolished nest, and I say: "I am not bound to my nest."

I see a son mourning for his father, and I say: "I am not bound to my parents."

I see a fish expiring as soon as it is taken out of the water, and I say: "That is me! If they take me out of Your embrace, I shall die in seconds—like a fish tossed onto the sand."

Yet how could I have plunged so far into You, with no way back, and lived, if I had not been in You before? Truly, I was in You from Your first awakening, because I sense that You are my home.

Eternity exists in eternity just as duration exists in time. In one eternity, O Lord, You were in ineffable sameness and Your vesperal blessedness. At that time Your hypostases were the truth within You, for it was impossible for them not to be in You. But they did not recognize one another, for they were unconscious of their diversity. In a second eternity You were in Your matinal blessedness, and the three hypostases recognized themselves as such.

The Father was not before the Son, nor was the Son before the Father, nor was the All-Holy Spirit before or after the Father and the Son. As a man while waking suddenly opens both eyes at the same time, so did the three hypostases within You suddenly open at the same time. There is no Father without the Son and no Son without the Holy Spirit.

When I lie beside my lake and sleep unconsciously, neither the power of consciousness, nor desire, nor action, die within me — rather they all flow into one blessed, nirvana-like, indistinguishable unity.

When the sun pours out its gold over the lake, I awaken not as a nirvana-like unity but as a triunity of consciousness, desire, and action.

This is Your history in my soul, O Lord, interpreter of my life. Is not the history of my soul the interpreter of the history of everything created, everything divided and everything united? And of You as well, my Homeland, my soul is—forgive me, O Lord — the interpreter of You.

O my Homeland, save me from the assaults of foreigners upon me.

O my Light, chase the darkness out of my blood.

O my Life, burn up all the larvae of death in my soul and my body.

XII

Anoint my heart with the oil of Your mercy, my most merciful Lord.

May neither anger against the strong nor scorning of the weak ever erupt in my heart! For everything is weaker than the morning dew.

May hatred never make a nest in my heart against those who plot evil against me, so that I may be mindful of their end and be at peace.

Mercifulness opens the way to the heart of all creatures, and brings joy. Mercilessness brings fog to the fore, and creates a cramped isolation.

Have mercy on Your merciful servant, most Tender Hand, and reveal to me the mystery of Your mercy.

The Ultimate Man is the child of the Father's mercy and the Spirit's light.

All creation is merely a story about Him. The mighty suns in the heavens and the smallest drops of water in the lake cany in themselves one part of the story about Him. All the builders of heaven and earth, from the exceedingly mighty seraphim to rulers and the tiniest particle of dust, tell the very same story about Him, their fore-essence and fore-source.

What are all the things on the earth and the moon except the sun in stories? Truly, in this way all visible and invisible creation is the Ultimate Man in stories. Essence is simple, but there is no end or number to the stories about essence.

My neighbors, how can I tell you about essence, when you do not even understand stories.

Ah if you only knew how great the sweetness, the expanse, and the strength are, when one reaches the bottom of all the stories—there, where the stories begin and where they end. There, where the tongue is silent and where everything is told at once!

How boring all the lengthy and tedious stories of creatures become then! Truly, they become just as boring as it is for one who is accustomed to seeing lightning to hear stories about lightning.

Receive me into Yourself, O Only-Begotten Son, so that I may be one with You as I was before creation and the Fall.

Let my long and weary story about You end with a moment's vision of You. Let my self-deception die, that would have me think that I am something without You, that I am something else outside of You.

My ears are stuffed with stories. My eyes no longer seek to see any display of clothing but You, my essence, overladen with stories and clothing.

XIII

You do not ask much of me, my love. Indeed, people ask more.

I am wrapped in a thick wrapping of nonexistence that covers the eyes of my soul. You only ask my soul to take off her misty wrapping and open her eyes to You, my might and my truth. People ask my soul to wrap herself more and more thickly with heavier and heavier wrappings.

O help me, help me! Help my soul to attain freedom and lightness, to attain lightness and aerial wings, to attain aerial wings and fiery wheels.

Stories are long, too long; the moral is short - one word. Stories spill over into stories, the way the smooth face of my lake spills over from color to color. Where does the colorful overflowing of the water under the sun end, and where does the overflowing of stories into stories end?

Stories are long, too long; the moral is short-one word. You are that word, O Word of God. You are the moral of all stories.

What the stars write across heaven, the grass whispers on earth. What the water gurgles in the sea, fire rumbles beneath the sea. What an angel says with his eyes, the imam shouts from his minaret. What the past has said and fled, the present is saying and fleeing.

There is one essence for all things; there is one moral for all stories. Things are tales of heaven. You are the meaning of all tales. Stories are Your length and breadth. You are the brevity of all stories. You are a nugget of gold in a knoll of stone.

When I say Your name, I have said everything and more than everything:

O my love, have mercy on me!

O my Might and Troth, have mercy on me!

XIV

What is clothing worth, if there is no body to clothe? What is the body worth, if the soul is not covered with it? What is the soul worth, If You do not keep vigil in it, like fire in ashes?

My clothing is smoke and ashes, if my body does not give it value.

My beautiful lake is blind mud, if its wide-eyed water is drained from it.

My soul is smoke and ashes, if You, my morning Dew, are drained from her.

You write Your name over the ashes of all things, and the flame of Your radiance dazzles the smoke of all things.

Your flame is a dew for the thirsty, who find refuge in Your embrace. But Your flame is a consuming fire for those who flee from it.

Truly, You are paradise for the pure and hell for the impure.

When the last Day comes--when the First and last Day shall be revealed as the One Day--the pure shall rejoice, but the impure shall mourn. And the impure shall cry out: "Alas, we ate ashes on earth, and now we must eat fire in heaven!"

Your prophets, O heavenly Mother, were the discoverers of the fire beneath the ashes, who dove into the mouths of volcanoes. Through Your boundless mercy You allowed each prophet to discover the spark for which he dove, until all the sparks merged into the blazing conflagration of Your Son, O heavenly Mother.

O Lord, You raised up shepherds for every flock, and the shepherds kindled fires for their flocks, lest they freeze on the rugged road of history, leading to the time when the Ultimate Man, the Only-begotten Son[2], would burst into a great fire and summon all the flocks to warm themselves.

Indeed how deeply hidden are all the precious metals--the eyes of the depths of the earth! Just as You are concealed beneath the ashes of the world, O most precious Stone!

The poor man plows his field and shakes his head when I say to him: "Rich man, deep beneath your barren field lies a lake of molten gold."

Do not shake your heads, impoverished sons of the King, when I tell you that the body is more precious than

---

[2] Cf. Phil. 2:9.11.

clothing, the soul is more precious than the body, and the Blazing King is more precious than the soul.

XV

White doves fly over my blue lake, like white angels over the blue heaven. The doves would not be white nor would the lake be blue, if the great sun did not open its eye above them.

O my heavenly Mother, open Your eye in my soul, so that I may see what is what--so that I may see who is dwelling in my soul and what sort of fruits are growing in her.

Without Your eye I wander hopelessly through my soul like a wayfarer in the night, in the night's indistinguishable gloom. And the wayfarer in the night falls and picks himself up, and what he encounters along the way he calls "events."

You are the only event of my life, O lamp of my soul. When a child scurries to the arms of his mother, events do not exist for him. When a bride races to meet her bridegroom, she does not see the flowers in the meadow, nor does she hear the rumbling of the storm, nor does she smell the fragrance of the cypresses or sense the mood of the wild animals--she sees only the face of her bridegroom; she hears only the music from his lips; she smells only his soul. When love goes to meet love, no events befall it. Time and space make way for love.

Aimless wanderers and loveless people have events and have history. Love has no history, and history has no love.

When someone makes their way down a mountain or climbs up a mountain without knowing where he is going, events are imposed upon him as though they were the aim of his journey. Truly, events are the aim of the aimless and the history of the pathless.

Therefore the aimless and the pathless are blocked by events and squabble with events. But I tranquilly hasten to You, both up the mountain and down the mountain, and despicable events angrily move out of the way of my footsteps.

If I were a stone and were rolling down a mountain, I would not think about the stones against which I was banging, but about the abyss at the bottom of the steep slope.

If I were a mountain stream, I would not be thinking about my uneven course, but about the lake that awaited me.

Truly terrifying is the abyss of those who are in love with the events that are dragging them downward.

O heavenly Mother, my only love, set me free from the slavery of events and make me Your slave.

O most radiant Day, dawn in my soul, so that I may see the aim of my tangled path.

O Sun of suns, the only event in the universe that attracts my heart, illuminate my inner self, so that I may see who has dared to dwell there besides You--so that I may eradicate from it all the fruits that seem sweet from the outside, but smell rotten in their core.

XVI

Arise O sons of the Sun of God! Arise, the merciful sun has risen and has begun to pour its light lavishly over the dark fields of the earth. It has risen to set you free from sleep's gloom and terror.
Your sins of yesterday are not written out on the sun. The sun does not remember or seek revenge for anything. On its face there are no wrinkles from your forehead, nor is there any sadness, envy, or sorrow. Its joy lies in giving, its youth-- its rejuvenation -- lies in serving. Blessed are those who serve, for they shall not grow old.

What if the sun were to imitate you, my neighbors? How little light it would shed on earth, you misers! How bloody its light would be, you murderers! How green it would become with envy when it saw greater suns that itself, you envious people! How red with wrath it would become when it heard the profanities below, you short-tempered people! How yellow it would become with yearning for the beauty of the stars, you greedy people! How pale it would become with fear, if no one marked its way, you cowards! How dark it would become with worry, you worrisome worriers! How wrinkled and old it would become living on yesterday's wrongdoing, you vengeful people! How astray it would go from the right way if it fought over rights, you auctioneers of rights! How cold and dead it would become, and how it would envelop the entire universe with its death, you preachers of death!

Oh how fortunate it is for the world that the sun will never imitate you, O sons and daughters of earth!

Indeed, the sun does not know many things as you do, but it does know two things eternally: that it is a servant and a symbol. It knows that it is a servant of the One who kindled it and that it is a symbol of the One who put it at His service.

Be servants of the One who illuminates you with the sun on the outside and with Himself on the inside, and you will taste the sweetness of eternal youth.

Be a symbol of the One who put you among the animals of the earth, and you will surpass the radiance of the sun. Truly all the animals around you will swim in happiness beneath the rays of your goodness, even as moons swim around suns.

Yet what are the sun and all the stars except piles of ashes, through which You shine, O Son of God? Piles of ashes that lessen Your radiance and sift it through themselves like a thick sieve? For indeed, in Your full radiance nothing would be seen except You, just as in total darkness nothing is seen except darkness.

O Lord, Lord, do not scorch us with Your radiance, which is unbearable for our eyes; and do not leave us in the gloom where one grows old and decays.
You alone know the measure of our needs, O Lord, glory to You!

XVII

How tedious to me are the counsels of human leaders and wise men--oh how tedious they seem to me--ever since Your wisdom caused my heart and mind to tremble, Holy God.
Those whom the dark desires of the heart are dragging into the abyss do not believe in Your light. There are no obstacles for a stone while it is rolling down a hill. The higher the steep slope and the deeper the abyss -- the swifter and more unrestrained is the rolling of the stone. One dark desire lures another with its success; and that one hires yet another, until all that is good in a person withers, and all that is evil gushes out in a torrential flood--until, along with everything else, all that the Holy Spirit has built is washed away, both inside and out;
Until the scorners of the light begin to scorn themselves and their teachers;
Until the sweetest sweets begin to choke them with their stench;
Until all the material goods, for which they killed neighbours and razed cities, begin to mock their monstrosity.

Then they stealthily lift their eyes toward heaven, and through the dung of their profaned and putrid existence, they cry out: "Holy God!"

How it irritates me like a burning arrow to hear men boasting of their power, ever since I came to know of Your powerful hand, Holy Mighty!

They build towers of stone and say: "We are better builders than your God." But I ask them: "Did you, or your fathers, build the stars?"

They discover light inside the earth, and boast: "We know more than your God." But I ask them: "Who buried the light beneath the earth for you to discover?"

They fly through the air and arrogantly say: "By ourselves we have created wings for ourselves, where is your God?" But I ask them: "Who gave you the idea of wings and flying if not the birds, which you did not create?"

Yet see what happens when You open their eyes to their own frailty! When irrational creatures show them their monstrous power; when their mind becomes filled with wonder at the starry towers, that stand in space without pillars or foundations; when their heart becomes filled with fear of their own frailty and insanity--then, in shame and humility, they stretch out their arms toward You and cry: "Holy Mighty!"

How it saddens me to see people overrating this life, ever since I tasted the sweetness of Your immortality, Holy Immortal!

The shortsighted see only this life, and say: "This is the only life there is, and we shall make it immortal by means of our deeds among men." But I tell them: "If your beginning is like a river, then it must have a source; if it is like a tree, it must have its root, if it is like a beam of light, it must come from some sun." And again I tell them: "So, you intend to establish your immortality among mortals? Try starting a fire in water!"

But when they look death in the face, they are left speechless, and torment seizes their heart. When they smell the flesh of their dead brides; when they leave the empty faces of their friends in the grave; when they place their hands on their sons' chests that have grown cold; when they realize that even kings are not able to buy off death with their crowns, nor heroes with their mighty deeds, nor wise men with their wisdom--then they feel the icy wind of death breathing down their necks too, and they fall down on their knees and bow their heads over their toppled pride, and pray to You: "Holy Immortal, have mercy on us!"

XVIII

Repent of your ways, inhabitants of the earth. Behold, the eye of the Master of the world is keeping watch deep within you. Do not trust your seducible eyes, let the Eye illumine your way. Your eyes are curtains over the Eye of God.

Repentance is admission of the way of sin. Repentance opens up a new way. The penitent's eyes are open to two ways: to the way which he is going, and to the way he should be going.

There are more who feel repentant than there are who turn their wheels onto a new way. I tell you: the penitent must have two types of courage--he must have the courage to weep over his old way, and he must have the courage to prepare himself for a new way.

What good is it for you to feel repentant and still tread the old way? How do you describe a person who is drowning and shouts for help, but when help arrives will not grab hold of the life line? I liken such a person to you.

Repent of your yearning for this world and all that is in this world. For this world is the graveyard of your ancestors, which is gaping and waiting for you. Just a little longer and you will be ancestors and will yearn to hear the word "repentance," but you will not hear it.

Just as the wind begins blowing and carries off the mist before the sun, so will death carry you off before the face of God.

Repentance rejuvenates the heart and lengthens one's lifetime. The tears of a penitent wash darkness from his eyes, and give his eyes a childlike radiance. The eye of my lake is like the eye of a deer, always moist and radiant as a diamond. In truth, the moisture in the eyes drains the anger in the heart.

The soul in the penitent is like a new moon. A full moon must wane, a new moon must wax.

The penitent clears the weeds from the field of his soul, and the seed of goodness begins to grow.

Truly, the penitent is not one who laments over the evil deed he has committed, but one who laments over all the evil deeds that he is capable of committing. A wise landowner not only cuts the thornbush that has pricked him, but every thornbush on the field that is waiting to prick him.

O my Lord, make haste to show a new way to every penitent, after he scorns his old way.

O heavenly Mother, Bride of the All-Holy Spirit, bow down toward our heart, when we repent. Open the fountain of tears within us, that we may wash away the heavy clay, that saddens our eyes.

O All-Holy Spirit, blow and disperse the unclean stench from the soul of the penitent that has been choking him and lead him to repentance.
We bow down and beseech You, O Life-giving and Mighty Spirit!

XIX

Amidst the racket and ridicule of people my prayer rises toward You, O my King and my Kingdom. Prayer is incense, that ceaselessly censes my soul and raises it toward You, and draws You toward her.

Stoop down, my King, so that I may whisper to You my most precious secret, my most secret prayer, my most prayerful desire. You are the object of all my prayers, all my searching. I seek nothing except You, truly, only You.
What could I seek from You, that would not separate me from You? Should I seek to be Lord over a few stars, instead of reigning as Lord with You over all the stars?

Should I seek to be first among men? How shameful it would be fore me, when You would seat me at the last place at Your table![3]

---

[3] Cf. Luke 14:7-10.

Should I seek for millions of human mouths to praise me? How horrible it would be for me, when all those mouths are filled with earth.[4]

Should I seek to be surrounded by the most precious objects from the entire world? How humiliating it would be for me for those objects to outlast me and be glistening even as earthen darkness fills my eyes![5]

Should I seek for You not to separate me from my friends? Ah separate me, O Lord, separate me from my friends as soon as possible, because they are the thickest wall between You and me.

"Why should we pray," say my neighbors, "when God does not hear our prayers?" But I say to them: "Your prayer is not prayer, but peddling merchandise. You do not pray to God to give you God but Satan. Therefore, the Wisdom of heaven does not accept the prayers from your tongue."

"Why should we pray," grumble my neighbors, "when God knows what we need beforehand?" But I sadly answer them: "That is true, God knows--that you need nothing except Him alone. At the door of your soul He is waiting to come in.[6] Through prayer the doors are opened for the entrance of the majestic King. Does not one of you say to the other at your door: 'Please enter'?

"God does not seek glory for Himself but for you. All the worlds in the universe can add nothing to His glory, much less can you. Your prayer is a glorification of you, not of God. Fullness and mercy are to be found in Him.

---

[4] Cf. John 12:43.
[5] Matt. 6:19-21.
[6] Cf. Rev. 3:20.

All the good words that you direct to Him in prayer, return to you twofold."

O my illustrious King and my God, to You alone I bow down and pray. Flood into me, as a raging stream into thirsty sand. Just flood me with Yourself, life-giving Water; then grass will easily grow in the sand and white lambs will graze in the grass.

Just flood into my parched soul, my Life and my Salvation.

XX

Think of yourself as though you were dead, I say to myself, and you will not feel the coming of death. Blunt the barb of death during life, and when it comes it will not have the means to sting.

Think of yourself every morning as a newborn miracle, and you will not feel old age.

Do not wait for death to come, because death has indeed already come and has not left you. Its teeth are continually in your flesh. Whatever was living before your birth and whatever will survive your death--that even now is alive within you.

One night an angel unwound the tape of time, the end of which I was unable to perceive, and he showed me two dots on the tape, one next to the other. "The distance between these two dots," he said, "is the span of your lifetime."

"That means my lifetime is already over," I shouted, "and I must be prepared for the journey. I must be like a diligent hostess, who spends the present day cleaning house and making preparations for tomorrow's *slava*[7] celebration."

Truly, the present day of all the sons of men is for the most part filled with concern for the next day. Yet few of those, who believe in Your promise, concern themselves with what will happen the day after death. May my death, O Lord, be my last sigh not for this world, but for that blessed and eternal Tomorrow.

Among the burned out candles of my friends, my candle, too, is burning down. "Do not be foolish," I reprimand myself, "and do not regret that your candle is burning out. Do you really love your friends so little, that you are afraid to set out after them, after the many who have strolled away? Do not regret that your candle is burning low, but that it is leaving behind unclear and dim light."

My soul has become accustomed to leaving my body every day and every night, and to stretch herself out to the limits of the universe. When she has sprouted in this way, my soul feels as though suns and moons are swimming over her even as the swans swim over my lake. She shines through suns and supports life on earthly planets. She supports mountains and seas; she controls thunder and winds. She completely fills

---

[7] slava - - (Serbian word meaning "glory") in Serbian Orthodox religious tradition, the rites performed with special bread (kolach) and wine in order to glorify one's patron saint on his feast day, usually accompanied by a sumptuous meal and large number of guests in one's home.

Yesterday, Today, and Tomorrow.[8] And she returns to shelter in a cramped and dilapidated habitation on one of those earthly planets. She returns to the body that she still, for another minute or two, calls her own, and which sways like her shadow among mounds of graves, among lairs of beasts, among howls of false hopes.

I do not complain about death, O Living God, it does not seem to me to be anything sad. It is a terror that man has created for himself. More strongly than anything on earth, death is pushing me to meet You.

I had a walnut tree in front of my house, and death took it from me. I was angry at death and cursed it saying: "Why did it not take me, an insatiable animal, instead of something sinless?"

But now I think of myself as though I were dead, and near my walnut tree.

O my Immortal God, look mercifully upon a candle that is burning out, and purify its flame. For only a pure flame rises toward Your face, and enters Your eye, with which you watch the whole world.

XXI

O heavenly Mother, receive me into Your glory. For when worldly glory is overtaken by darkness, it never dawns. And the crown that men bestow is always a crown of thorns for those who are rational and a

---

[8] "Jesus Christ is the same yesterday, today, and forever" (Heb. 13:8).

madman's cap for those who are irrational. While gold is in the ground everyone likes it and searches for it. After it is set as a crown on a man's head, the darkness of envy and animosity blinds its radiance.

Turn me into hidden gold in Your most hidden treasury, so that no one may know about me except You. For as long as You know me I am known. As long as only people know me, my name is doubt.

Hide me from the evil eyes of the world, for they infuriate me. Keep me like a secret, that envy cannot detect. Be wiser than I, and reveal me to no one. Indeed, I used to have You like a most precious secret, and I revealed You to the world, and the world ridiculed me. For envy ridicules, when it cannot take away what it envies.

My friends, why do you partake of human glory to the point of intoxication, a glory that begins with song and ends with lying in the mire?

My friends, all the mouths that are singing your praises now know yet another, opposite song, that you will hear later.
Flee from the glory that resembles a tower built on the back of a whale, lest both enemies and friends laugh at you from the shore.

The unanimous glory that comes from men is the most inglorious, because it is indifferent.

If your glory is a reward from the people, then you are a day laborer who has been paid off, and tomorrow the people can throw you off their fields.

Truly, no new day recognizes your contract with a day gone by. Every day opens a new field and makes a new agreement.

If your glory is the work of your mighty arms, your days will be anger and your nights will be fear.

If your glory is the work of your wisdom, wisdom will be a castration of your glory and you will be unable to move.

If you call your glory your own, Heaven will punish you for lying and stealing.

Stroll with your glory through a cemetery and see whether the dead will glorify you.

In truth, you are already strolling through a cemetery, and you are receiving glory from mobile tombs. Who will glorify you, after the mobile tombs become immobile?

You will become very sad in the other world, when you hear what those who have been glorifying you in this world really think of you. O heavenly Mother, hide me far from the eyes of men and the tongues of men. Hide me where only Your eye penetrates and only Your word is heard.
I beseech You, my Eternal Beauty!

XXII

O Only Son of God, receive me into Your wisdom. You are the head of all the sons of men. You are their heavenly comprehension, illumination and jubilation.

You are the One who thinks the same goodness in all men: the same thought and the same light. A man recognizes another man through You. A man prophesies to another man through You. Through Your voice men hear each other. In Your language they understand. Truly, You are the Ultimate Man, for existentially all men are in You and You are in each.

You build the mind of man, and Your shadow demolishes it.
You have formed all forms, and You have stamped all of them with the seal of Your wisdom. You have fashioned all vessels from clay and have filled them all with the song and joy of the Holy Triunity, but Your shadow has dripped a drop of sorrow into each vessel, with which the sorrowful inscribe griefs on You.

O Majestic Lord! You dance on Your Mother's lap, quickened by the All-Holy Spirit. Direct my mind to Your mind, and with Your radiance cleanse it of sorrowful thoughts, of sorrowful forebodings, of sorrowful intentions. O my Majestic Lord!

You fill the whole soul of Your Mother, all Her virgin breast; and there is nothing in Your Mother's soul except You. You are Her radiance and Her voice, truly Her eye and Her song.

You are the pride of the Holy Spirit Lord--His activity and His fruit--His fascination and His admiration! You, my Majestic Lord, who dance on Your Mother's lap, quickened by the Holy Spirit!

You are the courage of the Holy Trinity, Its heroism and Its history. You dared to let one triune ray into chaos and darkness, and the world became--a miracle, that the eye can not see nor the ear hear, O Creator of the eye and the ear.

And this whole miracle is just a pale picture of You, just a copied and distorted likeness of You in pieces of a half-darkened mirror.[9]

My heart yearns for Your complete image, O Son of God. For it is bitterness to be a fragment of Your image, drifting in-securely on an ocean of darkness.

Shatter the narrowness of my soul, O expanse of the triradiate Godhead!

Illuminate my mind, O light of angels and creatures. Make my life logical, Most Wise logos of God. Make my soul a virgin, and be her eye and her song.

---

[9] Cf. Is. 64:4 and 1 Cor. 2:9.

XXIII

The chamber of my soul is not aired out, and You, O awesome Holy Spirit, are knocking at the door. Just a moment, while I air out my chamber from its unclean spirits, and I shall open the door for You. For if I[10] opened it as it is, You would not enter into a chamber full of bad odors and would withdraw from my door forever. Just one moment, I beseech You, my most important guest!

Ah my shame and my sorrow, how that one moment is being prolonged! Just a little longer and my whole lifetime on earth will find its place within that moment. Yet You patiently wait at the door, and listen to my breathing.

The uninvited guests within me are impudent, they are impudent and have multiplied exceedingly. If I try to open a window, they pull my hands back. If I set out for the door to feel Your life-giving presence, they bind my feet. They tie me by force of habit to their foul stench, so that I am afraid of what is fresh and shrink back from what is new. Ah if only I am not too late to open the door to You!

But behold, even at the price of this life of slavery, I will open wide all the windows and in the name of the Most Pure Virgin and Her Son I will chase out of myself all the malicious masters and tyrants of my soul. And when You enter, You will bring my corpse to life with Your life-giving breath, with Your youthful strength, with Your loving dew.

---

[10] Cf. 1 Cor. 3:12.

O Spirit of manly strength, of matinal plenitude and vesperal quietude--You who are lighter than sleep, swifter than wind, fresher than dew, sweeter than a mother's voice, brighter than fire, holier than all sacrifices, stronger than the universe, more alive than life--to You I pray and You I worship; become my companion on the rugged path to the eternal blessedness of the Triune Godhead.

O fiery Spirit, You are never separated from the Virginity of Eternity. Pierce my soul, cleanse her, illuminate her, per-fume her with heavenly incense, enter her and make her Your bride, so that the hymn of Divine wisdom may be conceived within her; so that the Eye of eternity may be opened within her.

You arise early and never sleep, teach me to keep watch vigilantly and to wait patiently.

XXIV

You pour Your holy oil into the stars, O Holy Spirit, and out of senseless conflagrations You make vigil lamps before the Glory of Heaven. Pour Yourself into my soul also, and out of a passionate conflagration make a vigil lamp before the heavens.

You stroll through fields of flowers without being heard, and You sprinkle the flowers with Your grace, so that the blood of the earth may not look through, but the beauty of God. Sprinkle the field of my soul with Your grace also, so that it may not be said that the field of my soul sprouted from the blood of the earth, but that it is adorned with the beauty of God.

You mingle with every heap of ashes and pour in life. Pour life into the ashes of my body also, so that I may live and glorify Your works.

You tame the fire and wind, and out of demons of fury You make servants of the Most High. Tame my pride and make me a servant of the Most High.

You are kind to the animals in the woods. Show kindness to me also, who am animalized by ignorance.

You fertilize every seed of life. You hover in every womb. You sit in the egg of a bird's nest and masterfully form a new miracle of life. Fertilize, I beseech You, the invisible seed of goodness within me also, and keep watch over it until it reaches maturity.

O Awesome and Almighty Spirit, by Your presence You turn a den of thieves into a haven of Heaven, and a terrifying universe into a temple of God. Descend into me also, I beseech You, and turn a handful of ashes into what You know how to do and can.

XXV

You souls of the dead, join me in glorifying the Heavenly Triad. What other way do you have to spend your time except either to cringe for fear far from God or to soar for joy close to God?

You have left behind your bodily ashes, your favorite concern, and now you only have to worry about your nakedness. Surely you realize now that the body does not give fragrance to the soul, but the soul to the body.

How difficult it is for a sinful soul when it is undiluted by flesh and unhidden by flesh! Truly, a wheel does not go into the mud by itself, but only if a coachman drives it there. Surely you realize now that the wheel became sullied by the coachman's own will. The wheel has received its payment, and the coachman will receive his.

You sinful souls, yearn no longer to return to the body, as though you could supposedly flee from the evil stench that is suffocating you where you are now. You would only bring that same stench back with yourselves, and would increase it in a new body.

You sinful souls, yearn no longer to enter the body, as though you could flee the fire that is roasting you and the smoke that is smothering you! You would only bring the fire and smoke with yourselves, and your body would not be your rescuer but your burnt offering.

Rather direct all your attention to the eternal Virginity of God, which can cast out the evil stench from you, and to the Son of the Virgin, who would illuminate you with the flame of the wisdom of the Trinity, and to the All-Holy Spirit, who would give you the strength and the wisdom to elevate you to the choirs of angels.

You purified souls, who smell more captivating than all the balsams on earth, do not separate yourselves from those of us still on earth, who for another hour or two are still wandering over your paths of suffering and your ashes. All those who are pure on earth will be pure in heaven also, and will be your companions, perfumed with the balsam of paradise and clothed in the whiteness of virginity.

Strengthen your love for us and your prayer for us. For between you and us is no partition other than the frail veil of our flesh. For even though you have gone ahead while we have remained behind, the path is the same and the city at the end of the path is the same.

You righteous souls, we pray to the Lord for you as well, so that He may make your passage to Him easy and swift. Even though we are weaker than you, we nevertheless pray to God for you. We pray out of the love with which our heart burns for you, even as a younger and weaker brother reaches out to help his older and stronger brother.

For just as younger and older brothers are one flesh in the eyes of the love that gave them birth, so also are we and you one flesh in the eyes of the exceedingly wise and exceedingly strong lQve of the Most High.

You countless flocks of souls of the dead, do not be distraught and confounded, and have no more regard for the cold island of life on earth, to which we, being few in number, are still stuck for another hour or two until we come to join you for the summer in warmer and brighter regions.

For all of you, both righteous and sinful, we who are halfdead, half-alive pray to the Mercy of Heaven, so that you may not be confounded, so that you may not be afraid and look back, but may, in the fullness of summer, head ever forward and ever higher--
     toward light and joy
     toward peace and plenitude.

XXVI

Arise all you creatures and serve the Living Lord who cares about you. Worship Him and serve Him, for no one greater than He has visited you in this vale of fear and tears.

Servants come and make themselves lords. The Lord came and made Himself a servant. Servile lords strive to Lord it over as many people and creatures as possible, while the lordly Servant strives to serve as many people and creatures as possible.[11]

Arise, O lilies of the field, and give off your fragrance, for His holy mouth mentioned your name.[12]

Arise, O stone and rock, and worship Him, for His holy feet walked over you.
Arise, O desert, and rejoice, for He sanctified you with His longest and most mysterious prayers.[13]

Arise, O wheat and grapevine, for He blessed you especially among all created things. Arise and bless Him.

Arise, O fish, and glorify the Lord, for He was hungry and you nourished Him.[14]

Arise, O water and skies, and serve Him, for by His power He cleansed you and calmed you.[15]

---

[11] Cf. Mt. 20:25-28.
[12] Cf. Mt. 6:28-29.
[13] Cf. Mt. 4:1-11.
[14] Cf. Lk. 24:3-43 and Jn. 21:1-14.
[15] Cf. Mt. 14:22-33.

Arise, O sycamore tree, and clothe yourself in silk, for in you He saw a sinner and saved him.[16]

Arise, O sheep and oxen, and be filled with awe, for in your lowly stable He was born.[17]

Arise, O birds, and sing, for He raised you up as an example for men.[18]

Arise, O oil, and burn before His throne, for when He was anointed with you He felt joyful and saved a sinful woman.[19]

Arise, O thorns and reed, and be filled with shame, for you caused Him pain.[20]

Arise, O iron and wood, and repent, for even unwillingly you caused Him torments on the cross.[21]

Arise, inhabitants of cities, and weep, for you did not believe in Him.[22]

Arise, O leaders of the people, and sprinkle yourselves with ashes, for you passed judgment over Him.[23]

Arise, O paupers, and embrace Him, for He is your wealth.[24]

---

[16] Cf. Lk. 19:1-10.
[17] Cf Lk. 2:1-20.
[18] Cf. Mt. 6:26 and Lk. 12:24.
[19] Cf. Lk. 7:3-50.
[20] Cf. Mk. 15:1-20.
[21] Cf. Mk. 15:21-32.
[22] Cf. Mt. 11:20-24 and 23:37-39.
[23] Cf. Mt. 26:1-5 and 57-68.
[24] Cf Mt. 5:3 and Lk. 4:18.

Arise, O kings, and lay down your crowns before Him, for He alone has taught you true wisdom concerning primacy and leadership.

Arise, O sinners, and start sobbing before Him, for only His hand does not cast a stone at you.[25]

Arise, O righteous, and be vigilant, for your loader is coming to you.

Arise, all you stars, and begin to dance, for your Lightgiver goes to visit you.

Arise, O universe, and begin to hum the Lord's hymn, for the living Lord who cares about you has entered you.

XXVII

Your birds awaken me in the morning, and the murmur of the lake lulls me to sleep in the evening. But it is not the birds that awaken me, nor the lake that lulls me to sleep, but You, O Lord, Master of the voice.

You lend Your voice to the birds and the midnight murmur to the lake. You have lent a voice to every throat, and have put a story into every creature. I am surrounded by Your heralds, as a student by many teachers, and I listen to them tirelessly from dawn until dusk.

O Lord, Master of the voice, speak more clearly through Your heralds!

---

[25] Cf. Jn. 8:1-11.

The sun speaks to me about the radiance of Your countenance, and the stars about the harmony of Your being. The sun speaks in one language, and the stars speak in a different language, but all the languages flow out of the same vocal cords. The vocal cords belong to You, and You uttered the first sound that began to tremble in the deafness and formlessness of nothingness, and it broke into countless sounds and heralds, as a thundercloud breaks into rain drops.

O Lord, Master of the voice, speak more clearly through Your heralds!

One exclamation escaped the breast of the Bride of God when She saw Your Son--a voice filled with a love that could not be contained in silence. And that exclamation echoed in the heart of Her Son, and this echo--this response to the love of His Mother--the Holy Spirit has spread with His powerful arms throughout the entire universe. Therefore, all the universe is filled with Your heralds, O my Song and my love.

O Lord, Master of the voice, speak more clearly through Your heralds!

For this reason You also spoke in parables, O Son of God, and You would explain things and events as stories about the Most High God. You cured the sick with words and raised the dead with words, for You recognized the mystery of love. And the mystery of love is a mystery of words. Through all creatures, as through piercing and blaring trumpets, words pour forth--and through words, the love of Heaven.

O Lord, Master of the voice, teach me Your love through all Your heralds.

XXVIII

I feel mute and inarticulate, my Luxurious Lord, when I want to express Your stability and all Your fullness. Therefore, I beseech the entire universe to kneel down with me and speak in my stead, since I am incapable and inarticulate.

I build stone altars for You, O stone Foundation of my hope. And the arrogant sons of the world, who pretend to be nearer neighbors to You than Your saints, ridicule me: "Look at the pagan, who would rather worship stone than the Lord!"

Truly, I am not worshiping stone, but rather I, together with stone, am worshiping the Living Lord. For stone is also distant from the Lord and is in need of salvation. Sin has made me more impure than stone before the face of Heaven. May the stone be saved together with me, and may it, as a symbol of stability help my feeble words to express the stability of God's justice. Therefore, I embrace stone as a companion in the Fall and as a companion in prayer and salvation.

I light oil and wax on the stone altar, O Inextinguishable Light. And the arrogant puff themselves up and exclaim: "Look at the superstitious man, who does not know that God is spirit!"

Your servant, O Lord, knows that You are spirit, but he also knows of Your mercy towards all flesh. And so when I see the radiant oil and fragrant wax, I say to myself: "How are you better than oil or wax? Oil and wax at midnight, like the sun at noon, represent the glory of the Lord more clearly than your tongue. Let them be your help in prayer. Let them be your companions in prayer and salvation."

I adorn Your altar with wooden icons, golden crosses, silver seraphim, silk brocades, and books of salvation bound in leather. And I prostrate myself before Your embellished altars. But the arrogant laugh at me and say: "Look at the idol-worshiper, who does not worship the Lord but mute objects!"

Nevertheless, You know, my only Idol, that I am worshiping You alone. But so that arrogance may not engulf my heart and delay my salvation, I call upon tree and plant, resins and animals, to cry out together with me to You, each in its own language. Indeed, all creatures and all creation are in need of salvation, therefore, all also need to join in prayer with man, who led creation into sin and leads it to salvation.

I consecrate bread and wine on Your altar, and I nourish my soul with them. Let the arrogant ridicule me to the end of time, and I shall not be ashamed of my desire to have You for my food and drink, O my Life-giving Nourishment.

I worship before an altar of stone, so that I may learn to consider the entire universe the altar of the Most High.

I nourish myself with consecrated bread and wine at Your altar, so that I may learn to consider everything I eat to be Your holy body, and everything I drink to be Your holy blood.

I pray with all creation and for all creation, so that I may learn humility before You, and so that I may express all the mystery of my love for You, O all-embracing Love.

XXIX

For all the sins of men I repent before You, Most Merciful Lord. Indeed, the seed of all sins flows in my blood! With my effort and Your mercy I choke this wicked crop of weeds day and night, so that no tare may sprout in the field of the Lord, but only pure wheat.[26]

I repent for all those who are worried, who stagger under a burden of worries and do not know that they should put all their worries on You. For feeble man even the most minor worry is unbearable, but for You a mountain of worries is like a snowball thrown into a fiery furnace.

I repent for all the sick, for sickness is the fruit of sin. When the soul is cleansed with repentance, sickness disappears with sin, and You, my Eternal Health, take up Your abode in the soul.

I repent for unbelievers, who through their unbelief amass worries and sicknesses both on themselves and on their friends.

I repent for all those who blaspheme God, who blaspheme against You without knowing that they are blaspheming against the Master, who clothes them and feeds them.

---

[26] For the parable of the wheat and the tares, see Matt. 13:24-30.

I repent for all the slayers of men, who take the life of another to preserve their own. Forgive them, Most Merciful[27] Lord, for they know not what they do. For they do not know that there are not two lives in the universe, but one, and that there are not two men in the universe, but one. Ah, how dead are those who cut the heart in half!

I repent for all those who bear false witness, for in reality they are homicides and suicides.

For all my brothers who are thieves and who are hoarders of unneeded wealth I weep and sigh, for they have buried their soul and have nothing with which to go forth before You.

For all the arrogant and the boastful I weep and sigh, for before You they are like beggars with empty pockets.

For all drunkards and gluttons I weep and sigh, for they have become servants of their servants.

For all adulterers I repent, for they have betrayed the trust. of the Holy Spirit, who chose them to form new life through them. Instead, they turned serving life into destroying life.

For all gossipers I repent, for they have turned Your most precious gift, the gift of speech, into cheap sand.

For all those who destroy their neighbor's hearth and home and their neighbor's peace I repent and sigh, for they bring a curse on themselves and their people.

---

[27] Cf. Luke 23:34.

For all lying tongues, for all suspicious eyes, for all raging hearts, for all insatiable stomachs, for all darkened minds, for all ill will, for all unseemly thoughts, for all murderous emotions--I repent, weep and sigh.

For all the history of mankind from Adam to me, a sinner, I repent; for all history is in my blood. For I am in Adam and Adam is in me.

For all the worlds, large and small, that do not tremble before Your awesome presence, I weep and cry out: O Master Most Merciful, have mercy on me and save me!"

XXX

Blot out, O Lord, all my memories--except one. For memories make me old and feeble. Memories ruin the present day. They weigh down the present day with the past and weaken my hope in the future, for in legions they whisper in my ear: "There will only be what has already been."

But I do not wish for there to be only what has been. I do not wish and You do not wish, O Lord, for the future to be the past repeated. Let things happen that have never appeared before. The sun would not be worth much, if it only watched repetitions.

Worn paths mislead a wayfarer. Earth has walked over the earth a long time. Earthly walkways have become boring, for they have been traveled again and again from generation to generation throughout all time. Blot out, O Lord, all my memories except one.

Just one memory do I ask You not to blot out, but to strengthen in me. Do not blot out but strengthen in my consciousness the
memory of the glory that I had when I was entirely with You and entirely in You, before time and temporal illusions.

When I, too, was a harmonious trinity in holy unity, just as You are from eternity to eternity.

When the soul within me was also in friendship with consciousness and life.

When my soul also was a virginal womb, and my consciousness was wisdom in virginity, and my life was spiritual power and holiness.

When I, too, was all light, and when there was no darkness within me.

When I, too, was bliss and peace, and when there were no torments of imbalance within me.

When I also knew You, even as You know me, and when I was not mingled with darkness.

When I, too, had no boundaries, no neighbors, no partitions between "me" and "you."

Do not blot out this memory, my Father, but strengthen it. Even if it reveals to me the abyss along which I am journeying in humbleness and nothingness.

Even if it separates me from friends and pleasantries, and demolishes all the barriers between Yesterday, Today, and Tomorrow.[28]

Even if it leads me outside of myself, and makes me seem mad in the eyes of my fellow wayfarers.

In truth, no companionship pleases me except Yours, and no memory pleases me except the memory of You.

O my Merciful Father, blot out all my memories except one alone.

XXXI

You pour out light over the darkness, Lord, and colors and shapes emerge. You bend Your face over the abyss, whose name is Nothingness, and the abyss tries to depict the beauty of Your face in shadows. All creation expresses You the way the abyss dreams of You.

My lake is also beautiful while the peaceful face of the sun remains bent over it. And all those who pass by praise the beauty of my lake. But as soon as the sun hides its face, my lake becomes dark and abysmal. And no passerby ever offers any praise for the lake except in the presence of the sun or the sun's radiant companions.

The face of the abyss intoxicates those who do not see the sun bent over the abyss. The beauty of things begins when an onlooker bends his face over them. There is no

---

[28] "Jesus Christ is the same yesterday, today, and forever" (Heb. 13:8).

mirror if there is no face in front of the mirror. But even a face in front of a mirror means nothing if there is no light.

In the light of Your face I pay no attention to any creature. Without You, creatures and I would not be mirrors of one another, but rather darkness, and an abyss, and an opaque chill.

Creation distorts Your beauty the way a dream distorts reality. Creation torments me just as dreams torment me. For what is creation except dreams of Your inexpressible Reality?

My neighbors say: "We have dreamed beautiful dreams." The universe is my witness when I tell you that you are more beautiful than your dreams. The universe also dreams, and cannot dream enough about its own beauty. O my sleepy universe: as long as a dream dreams a dream, one dream is afraid of another, even if one dream seeks an interpreter and comforter in another. Who is prophesying to whom: the dream to reality or reality to the dream?

O my beautiful universe: dream of Reality and Reality will tell you everything. Admit the Reality, of which you are a dream, and you will awaken, and will no longer ramble about beauty, but will be Beauty. There is only one Reality and only one Beauty, and it is the reason for your dream.

Do not tell me, children, about the beauty of the stars. If the Lord withdrew Himself from the stars, your mouths would be struck dumb. Stand in the thick darkness by my lake and try to sing to it. Truly you will be struck dumb and remain silent until the sun dawns, until the sun pours its beauty over the lake and gives your speechless throat its voice.

Your face pours beauty over all creation. The universe swims in Your beauty as a boat swims in the sea.

And when You bend over cold ashes, the ashes are transfigured and receive a face.

Bring my heart to its senses, my Lord, so that it may not be captivated by mortal beauty but by You, my Immortal Beauty.

O my only Beauty!

Allow me to see Your Face, just more and more--of Your Face.

XXXII

My faith sees You, Lord.

It is the light and the farseeing vision of my eyes.

It is the sensing of Your omnipresence. It pulls my knees to the ground and lifts my arms toward heaven.

My faith is my soul's contact with You. It prompts my heart to dance and my throat to sing.

When a swallow draws near, the baby swallows become excited in the nest. For even in the distance they sense the coming of their mother.

My faith is my excitement, for You are coming, my Mother.

If my friend is thinking of me while writing a letter in a distant city, I also dismiss other thoughts and think of my friend.

My faith is my thinking about You, which prompts You, all-encompassing Lord, to think of me.

When a lion is separated from his lioness, the lion's eyes are distraught with longing for the lioness.

My faith is my longing for You, when You are far from me, my Beauty.
When there is no sun, the most terrifying storms lash the sea.

My faith is the calming of the storm within my soul, for Your light pours into me and pacifies me.

My eyes said to me: "We do not see Him." But I pacified them with the words: "The truth is, that you were not created to see Him but to see what is His."

My ears said to me: "We do not hear Him." But I brought them to their senses with the words: "The truth is, that you were not created to hear Him but to hear what is His."

Nothing of all that is created can see or hear Him but only what is His. What is created sees and hears what is created. Only what is begotten of Him can see Him. And only what is begotten of Him can hear Him. A painting cannot see the painter, but the son of a painter can see the painter. A bell cannot hear a bell-caster, but the daughter of a bell-caster can hear her father.

The eye cannot see Him because it was not created for the purpose of seeing Him. The ear cannot hear Him, because it was not created for the purpose of hearing Him. But vision can see Him, and hearing can hear Him.

My faith sees You, Lord, just as what is begotten sees its begetter. My faith hears You, Lord, just as what is begotten hears its begetter.

The God within me sees and hears the God in You. And God is not created but begotten.

My faith is like diving into the abyss of my soul and swimming out with You.

My faith is my only genuine knowledge. Everything else is like the children collecting motley pebbles by the lake.

XXXIII

My hope awaits You, Lord.

Expecting You is the only content and meaning of my Tomorrow and the Day after Tomorrow.

The grass expects the dew and is not disappointed. The mountain expects the thunder, and is not disappointed. The mole in the ground expects its meal, and is not disappointed. You fulfill the expectations of all beings.

I am expecting You, and You are coming to meet me. With the same haste that I am approaching You, You are coming toward me.

What is Tomorrow, children of earth, except your hope. If you eradicate all your hope, your desire to see Tomorrow dawn will die.

Do not grumble against Heaven because It does not fulfill all your hopes. Grumble against yourselves, because you do not know how to hope. Heaven does not fulfill hopes but hope. The most sublime and steadfast hope Heaven always fulfills. Do not grumble against Heaven because It does not see the benefits for your family and your factions and enter into your intrigues against one another. Heaven is discerning and merciful. It is discerning for anything good in any faction, and is merciful towards your infirmity, provided that good will accompanies it.

My hope is not an inkling but a certainty that You will come. You promised, and I bear the seal of Your promise in my soul. If You have not come yet, it is not Your fault but mine. You are tender and compassionate, and would not wish to make me ashamed of my unpreparedness. Therefore, You approach slowly, and continuously announce Your coming.

Hopelessness sits idle. But my hope cleans and washes continuously; it airs out and censes the quarters where it will receive You. And it frets day and night lest it forget anything whatsoever that might be pleasing to You. And it continuously calls upon the angels and the saints, the mystery-seers, to show it how to make its cave like Heaven.

My hope has no other partners. I have chased out of myself all other hopes as proven imposters. And now in their place there sprouts only one hope, which awaits You.

When You come You will bring me the richest gifts. With You, O Victorious One, will come my victory over all boredoms and worries. With You will come light, and health, and strength, and wisdom and the complete fulfillment of all human expectations from the beginning to the end of time.

In truth, the people with many hopes, that exclude You, sit on the mountain and wait for the sun to rise from the West.

But I stand facing the East, and I know for certain that the sun will soon be born. For I see the dawn becoming rosy.

Others plant dry rods in the ground, and hope for greenery and fruit. But over my field I sowed living seed, which is turning green and bearing fruit.

My hope in You is not a myth but a certainty--as certain as the fact that the sun must rise from the East and that good seed, when sown on good soil, must sprout.

The field is Yours, and You are the sower and the seed.

Come, O Lord, my hope awaits You!

XXXIV

Love makes me God, and You, O God, man.

Where there is one, there is no love. Where there are two united there is only a semblance of love. Where three are united, there is love. Your name is love because Your name is trinity in Unity.

If You were solitary, You would not be love but hatred.

If You were a duality, You would be an alternation of love and hatred. But You are a trinity, and therefore You are love, and in You there is neither darkness nor alternation.

Love knows neither time nor space. It is outside of time and outside of space. For love one day is like a thousand years and a thousand years like one day.
When I am united with You in love, neither heaven nor earth exists--only God exists. No "you" or "I" exists--only God exists.

Love has three hypostases: chastity, knowledge, and light. Without chastity love is not affection but selfishness and passion. Without knowledge love is not affection but selfishness and passion. Without knowledge love is not wisdom but foolishness. Without light love is not power but weakness. When passion, foolishness, and weakness combine, they become hell, which is what Satan likes to call "love."

When my soul is a most pure virgin, and my conscience is keen-sighted wisdom, and my spirit is life-giving light, I am a love that coincides with Your love.

Through love I see You in myself, and You see me in Yourself.

Through love I do not see myself but only You. Through love You do not see Yourself but only me.

Love sacrifices itself, and does not feel that the sacrifice is giving but rather receiving.

My worldly children: the word "love" is the deepest prayer of all.

"Does worldly love not exist?" my neighbors ask me. "To the same extent that a worldly God exists," I answer. "Worldly love burns and burns out, Heavenly love burns without burning out. Worldly love, like everything worldly, is only a dream and semblance of love. Your love resembles divine love the way smoke resembles flames.

"When you exchange a gold coin for copper pennies, you do not call the pennies a gold coin but copper pennies. Why then do you call divine love that has been broken and ground into ashes by time and space 'love' and not 'ashes'?"

O Lord, make me worthy of the love, by which You live and give life.

Make me worthy of Your love, O Lord, and I shall be free of all laws.

Move Your love into me, and love will move me into You.

XXXV

Martyrs of the true faith, pray to God for us.

Your faith has brought you near to the radiant throne of glory, adorned with the shining seraphim and the overpowering cherubim. You are nearer to immortality than we, and your prayer is more pure and audible.

Remember us in your prayer also, so that you may be ever more acclaimed throughout heaven. Bring us with you also, and you will more swiftly and easily fly to the throne of glory. Whoever brings himself alone, walks more slowly and stumbles more often. The greater the load of your brothers you haul, the faster you fly.

I have said to people: You are all martyrs, but not all of one martyrdom. Martyrs for the true faith are not the same as martyrs for a false faith. Truly, their bones are similar but not the soul. For the soul transfers power and weakness even to the bones.

You who suffer for the true faith, are suffering for what your spiritual vision sees. You who suffer for a false faith, are suffering for what your physical eyes see. You former suffer for faith in reality and truth; you latter suffer for a dream and a fantasy.

Spiritual vision calls its knowledge by a humble name--faith. Physical eyes call their faith by a boastful name--knowledge. Both the one and the other are seeing: the first is a seeing of the peaceful and sparkling essence of creation; the second is a seeing of flickers of that essence through the darkness.

Your martyrdom is the most inevitable of all things, O sons of heaven and sons of earth. Your being martyred lies in your fleeing from light toward darkness. If you are fleeing from darkness toward light, you will stir up the world against yourself. If you are fleeing from light toward darkness, Heaven will remove itself from your convulsions and destruction.

The paths of the sons of men meet, and conflict is inevitable. For some are journeying toward the East, while the others are journeying toward the West. The Lord is merciful, and sends His angels to them all.

My soul is full of martyrs like a fertile field full of wheat and tares. The first are facing the East, while the others are facing the West.

I whisper to my soul at midnight: "How long will you be crucified between paradise and hell? Take hold of yourself, and face only the direction where the martyrs of the true faith have journeyed."

I whisper to my neighbor at dawn: "Do not take the heavily traveled road, for many stinking corpses are strewn along it. Let us take the trail up the mountain, which is rugged but does not reek of corpses."[29]

I whisper morning and evening to you, O martyrs of the true faith: "Pray to God for us."

---

[29] Cf Matt. 7:13-14.

XXXVI

Martyrs of good hope, pray to God for us.

You who have buried all hopes, so that you might be wealthy in a single hope;

Who have awaited the end of many human aspirations, and seen the ashes;

Who have seen many tear-stained eyes returning from the graveyard of their hopes;

Who have heard many confessions concerning the evil stench of every worldly hope from the other realm;

And who have permitted yourselves to be crucified[30] for one special hope, which does not end in ashes, nor in a graveyard, nor in an evil stench.

To you we bow down and pray: "Pray to God for us."

I saw a child chasing after a bird with dappled feathers and a golden beak for a long time, and when he caught it, the bird pecked him and the child began to cry.

I said: "Such are you with your hopes, human children, and such is your end."

Again I saw a child running after a swarm of spring butterflies for a long time, and when one butterfly was near him, he left it and ran off after the others, which seemed to him to be more beautiful.

---

[30] Cf. Rom. 6:6, Gal. 2:20 and 5:24.

I said: "Such are the sons of men, and such is their running through the whole of life after many desires."

Truly, your race is tiring and futile. If the hour of death comes upon you, you will not be able to say what it is that you have been pursuing. And you will enter into the other world with empty hands and a perplexed heart.

The race of the sons of heaven is also tiring, but is not futile. And when the hour of death comes upon them, they will be able to say what it is that they have been pursuing. And in the other world they will have full hands and a restful heart.

An eagle beneath the clouds sees a lamb in the field and descends toward it, and asks the sparrows perched on the back of the lamb: "Do you not see the lamb?" And they answer him: "No, we do not see it." So it is with martyrs of good hope. At a great distance they spot their nourishment, while those next to the nourishment are walking over it without seeing it.

The race for good hope is a long one. But a champion sets his mind on the race, and casts all illusory hopes beneath his feet and tramples over them like dry leaves. There are many, very many hurdles between him and his hope;--and death is one of the hurdles. But he leaps over them all; he even leaps over death, and pursues his hope.

Martyrs of good hope, who flutter around the Light of Heaven like a flock of white doves, pray to God for us.

XXXVII

Martyrs of great love, pray to God for us.

You who have known a love stronger than death, pray to Love for us.

You who in this life luckily escaped from the snare of transitory love, which is like a little color on a boulder, which the rain washes away;

You who have preached that love is more mysterious than the flesh, and more eternal than the stars in heaven;

You who through love have understood both wood and stone, both the beast in the forest and the fish in the water (for love breaks the seals of all mysteries, and all things appear naked to their lover);

You who with love have fulfilled all the prophets, satisfied all religions, and surpassed all laws;

You are the greatest of conquerors, who is stronger than you?

You are the greatest of wise men, who is wiser than you?

You are the greatest of precious stones, who is scarcer than you?

You are gods,[31] who have seen yourselves in God and God in yourselves.

---

[31] Cf. Ps. 82:6.

You have an honor greater than the angels, for the angels became angels without torment and martyrdom. To you we bow down and pray, pray to God for us.

That we too may cleanse ourselves of the illusory love, that ends in hatred.

That we too may crown our faith and hope with a crown in which even suns have little value.

That we too may begin to see, and know, and rejoice with the joy, with which only the angels can rejoice.

That our life may also become a triradiate splendor, like the One from whom all splendor, unmixed with darkness, comes.

That we too may recognize in ourselves the eternal virgin, and the pre-eternal Son of the Virgin, and the dove-like Spirit.

Martyrs of great love, only your suffering is less than your love. Every worldly love brings suffering greater than its love. But you have loved what is deeper than time and wider than space.

When your mortal brothers hear about your sufferings they consider them unbelievable and unbearable. For they can really imagine themselves only in your sufferings and not in your love, in the meaning of your sufferings. Oh, if they could only imagine themselves in your love also! All your sufferings would seem like nothing to them, just as they seemed to you. Just as the cold rain and the howling of the wind seem like nothing to a mother as she hurries home to her child.

To one who has a goal greater than the world, the world can do nothing.

One who hurries to a home wider than space, space cannot contain.

One who has a love more precious than temporal creations, can neither be impeded nor trampled by time.

Across all rugged terrain and through all stormy tempests Love leads His beloved ones and draws them to Himself.

Martyrs of great love, pray to God for us.

XXXVIII

You work wonders through created things, O Lord, while men have lost the gift of wonderworking.

You take fire and water for Your servants, while people refuse to serve You.

To wood and metal You give Your power, while it is returned to You, despised by people.

Through earth and grass You bestow mercy on Your chosen ones, while people make themselves too impure to be channels of mercy.

Through fabric and paper Your might shines, while human carnality dominates the spirit.

The bones of the saints proclaim Your name and Your presence, while the tongue of people has been struck dumb by disbelief.

When generals have forgotten how to achieve victory, You make the rank and file the victors.

You have filled dead objects with fire, so that they may shine, when darkness closes the eyes of the stars.

When there is no sun, the fern and the hawthorn assume the duty of shining.

When the blind begin to lead the blind,[32] You surrender the army to the horses and dogs.

When sick men foist themselves upon the sick as healers, You make healers out of dead bones and mud.

When Your image in the human soul vanishes, You give power and might to Your image in wood.

Those, who in the end will weep bitterly, laugh and say: "How can dead objects work wonders, which even we cannot work?"

Are these objects not alive, if You bring them to life? And are people not dead, if You abandon them, O Fearful Lord?

Your angels know, yet people do not know, that all powers are Yours, in You and from You, and that You manifest them through pure channels. What if a stone is

---

[32] Cf Matt. 15:14.

pure while a man is impure? Will not the Lord's might be manifested through the stone rather than through the man?

Only a righteous man laughs with the laughter of joy. The laughter of the unrighteous man is malice.

The unrighteous man laughs at the relics of the saints, and he is consumed by malicious laughter. Oh if he only knew that the dead relics of the saints contain more life than his own flesh and blood!
Truly, malice is distant from the Most Merciful Lord , just as malice is always distant from virginity, rationality and sanctity.

Indeed, the Logical Lord is always ready to do good to men through men. But when men become impure, and become bereft of logic and holiness, the All-Merciful rushes to help people through dead objects.

O All-Merciful and Longsuffering Lord, do not leave the world without channels of Your might and mercy.

XXXIX

Do you know, my child why the clouds are closed when the fields are thirsty for rain, and why they open, when the fields have no desire for rain?

Nature has been confused by the wickedness of men, and has abandoned its order.
Do you know, my child, why the fields produce heavy fruit in the springtime, and yield a barren harvest in the summer?

Because the daughters of men have hated the fruit of their womb, and kill it while it is still in blossom.

Do you know, my child, why the springs have gone dry, and why the fruits of the earth no longer have the sweetness that they used to have?

Because of the sin of man, from which infirmity has invaded all of nature.

Do you know, my child, why a victorious nation suffers defeats as a result of its own disunity and discord, and eats bread made bitter by tears and malice?

Because it conquered the bloodthirsty enemies around itself, but failed to conquer those within itself.

Do you know, my child, how a mother can feed her children without nourishing them?

By not singing a song of love to them while nursing them, but a song of hatred towards a neighbor.

Do you know, my child, why people have become ugly and have lost the beauty of their ancestors?

Because they have cast away the image of God, which fashions the beauty of that image out of the soul within, and removes the mask of earth.

Do you know, my child, why diseases and dreadful epidemics have multiplied?

Because men have begun to look upon good health as an abduction of nature and not as a gift from God. And what is abducted with difficulty must with double difficulty be protected.

Do you know, my child, why people fight over earthly territory, and are not ashamed to be on the same level as moles?

Because the world has sprouted through their heart, and their eyes see only what is growing in the heart; and because, my child, their sin has made them too weak to struggle for heaven.

Do not cry, my child, the Lord will soon return and set everything right.

XL

With prayer I cleanse the vision of my faith, lest it lose sight of you in the mist, O my Most Radiant Star.

"What use will your prayer be to God?" ask the swarthy workers of the earth.

You speak rightly, sons of earth. What use is the mariner's telescope to the North Star, when it sees the mariner even without a telescope? But do not ask me, since you already know, what use a telescope is to a mariner.

Prayer is necessary for me, lest I lose sight of the salvation-bearing Star, but the Star does not need it to keep from losing me.

What would become of my inner vision, if I were to stop training it with prayer?

Are the soldiers of the earth not trained, extensively and strenuously, to see targets in the distance?

Are weavers of silk not trained, extensively and strenuously, to recognize the finest fibers?

How could I not train the vision of my faith to see my sole treasure as clearly as possible?

Trapped in a web of illusions, I have barely caught sight of a way out, so do you really expect me to lose sight of it?
Get it into your heads, my fellow wayfarers, that seeing God is not a cheap affair. You who sacrifice fortunes to see the luxuriance of the tropics or the polar lights of the arctic, must pay more dearly to see the One for whom the luxuriance of the tropics is poverty and the polar lights are a tallow candle.

When you give even your entire life in order to see Him, you have barely paid a penny. Nevertheless He is magnanimous and good-hearted, and expects nothing more from you than this.

You who train your bodies, who every morning do not forget to exercise your arms and legs, your head and neck, are you in truth contemplative beings--you who are like samurai warriors? Are you in truth contemplative beings, if you maintain that your faith in God will become and remain clairvoyant without training? All the stars of Heaven, which have seen the experience of your fathers, bear witness to me that your faith will go blind, if indeed it had ever even begun to see at all. And in place of the lost blessing there will remain a hypocritical vision in name only.

Keep your eyes blindfolded for just three days, and afterward you will find that the light of the sun hurts them. Sever your bond with God for just three hours and you will find it painful to look at His light again.

You ask me: how long does my prayer last? Can you understand me when I tell you that it lasts longer than my days? For by my prayer I must train your faith also, and open its eyes, and show it how to see and whom it is seeing. Truly, I continuously fill both my days and yours with prayer.

I ceaselessly cense my faith with prayer, lest the scents of the world blind it.

I ceaselessly call upon all the celestial spheres to sustain me in my prayer for everlasting prayerfulness, so that I too may be deemed worthy to gaze upon that Glory and Beauty, which is wide open to their gaze.

Oh my fellow wayfarers, how majestic is the vision of faith! I swear to you, if you only knew how majestic it is, your prayer would never pause or end.

XLI

With fasting I gladden my hope in You, my Lord, Who are to come again.

Fasting hastens my preparation for Your coming, the sole expectation of my days and nights.

Fasting makes my body thinner, so that what remains can more easily shine with the spirit.

While waiting for You, I wish neither to nourish myself with blood nor to take life--so that the animals may sense the joy of my expectation.

But truly, abstaining from food will not save me. Even if I were to eat only the sand from the lake, You would not come to me, unless the fasting penetrated deeper into my soul.

I have come to know through my prayer, that bodily fasting is more a symbol of true fasting, very beneficial for someone who has only just begun to hope in You, and nevertheless very difficult for someone who merely practices it.

Therefore I have brought fasting into my soul to purge her of many impudent fiancé's and to prepare her for You like a virgin.

And I have brought fasting into my mind, to expel from it all daydreams about worldly matters and to demolish all the air castles, fabricated from those daydreams.

I have brought fasting into my mind, so that it might jettison the world and prepare to receive Your Wisdom.

And I have brought fasting into my heart, so that by means of it my heart might quell all passions and worldly selfishness.

I have brought fasting into my heart, so that heavenly peace might ineffably reign over my heart, when Your stormy Spirit encounters it.

I prescribe fasting for my tongue, to break itself of the habit of idle chatter and to speak reservedly only those words that clear the way for You to come.

And I have imposed fasting on my worries so that it may blow them all away before itself like the wind that blows away the mist, lest they stand like dense fog between me and You, and lest they turn my gaze back to the world.

And fasting has brought into my soul tranquility in the face of uncreated and created realms, and humility towards men and creatures. And it has instilled in me courage, the likes of which I never knew when I was armed with every sort of worldly weapon.

What was my hope before I began to fast except merely another story told by others, which passed from mouth to mouth?

The story told by others about salvation through prayer and fasting became my own.

False fasting accompanies false hope, just as no fasting accompanies hopelessness.

But just as a wheel follows behind a wheel, so true fasting follows true hope.
Help me to fast joyfully and to hope joyously, for You, my Most Joyful Feast, are drawing near to me with Your radiant smile.

XLII

My love keeps vigil and through vigil it never grows weary. The One, whom I love and whom I await, is coming to me surrounded by a heavenly retinue. How could I be sleeping, and how could vigil make me weary?

I keep vigil over the stories of men and the stories of things, in case I can discern some secret message of my Love. No story interests me by virtue of the story itself or because of the story-teller, but only on account of You.

I do so in the manner that a singer, who loses his own note, begins to listen attentively to everyone else's part, and attempts to recognize his own part. And everywhere he finds some note similar to his part, but nowhere his part completely.

I do so in the manner that a man, who shatters a glass mirror, then proceeds to see his own face in the faces of people, in the faces of animals, and in the faces of all things. And everywhere he finds some feature similar to his own face, but nowhere his face in its entirety.

Thus I too keep vigil over the innumerable voices of the entire universe. And I keep vigil over the innumerable faces in the universe, from the face of the white pebbles by the lake to the starry face of the Big and Little Dippers, to see whether I can recognize the face of my Love. And no one deceives me, rather each tells me whatever little he can of what he knows about You.

When I pose questions to people, I await answers from You. When things speak, I listen to You. When I look at nature, I am looking for You.

When people see me pensive, they suppose that I am thinking about them, while I am actually thinking about You. When they see me loving to labor, they think that I am laboring for people, but I am laboring for You.

When nature hears its name on my lips, it thinks that I am lauding it, but I am lauding You. When I feed a dove, I am offering it to You. When I hug a lamb, I am hugging You. When I smile at the sun, my smile penetrates through all the stars until it meets with Your smile. When I bow down to kiss the white lily, I am dropping my kiss through seven realms onto the footstool of Your feet.

The vigilance of my love goes side by side with the prayer of my faith and the fasting of my hope. And none of them rises

All the activity of my mind serves my faith.

All the activity of my heart serves my hope.

All the activity of my soul serves my love.[33]

When I feed a dove, I am offering it to You, my Love.

---

[33] Cf. 1 Cor. 13:13.

XLIII

People can do me no evil, as long as I have no wounds.

I saw two caves, one of which revealed an echo, while the other had none. And many curious children were visiting the former and were mischievously carrying out shouting matches with the cave. But from the other cave visitors were quickly returning, because it was not answering them with an echo.

If my soul is wounded, every worldly evil will resound within it. And people will laugh at me, and will throng more and more strongly with their shouting.

But truly, evil-speaking people will not harm me, if my tongue has forgotten how to speak evil.

Nor will external malice sadden me, if there is no malice in my heart to resound like a goatskin drum.

Nor shall I be able to respond to ire with ire, if the lair of ire within me has been vacated and there is nothing to be aroused.

Nor will human passions titillate me, if the passions within me have been reduced to ashes.

Nor will the unfaithfulness of friends sadden me, if I have resolved to have You for my friend.

Nor can the injustice of the world crush me, if injustice has been expelled from my thoughts.

Nor will the deceitful spirits of worldly pleasure, honor and power entice me, if my soul is like an immaculate bride, who receives only the Holy Spirit and yearns for Him alone.

People cannot shove anyone into hell, unless that person shoves himself. Nor can people hoist anyone up on their shoulders to the throne of God, unless that person elevates himself.

If my soul has no open windows, no mud can be thrown into it.
let all nature rise up against me; it can do nothing to me except a single thing--to become the grave of my body more swiftly.

Every worldly crop is covered with fertilizer, so that it will sprout as soon as possible and grow better. If my soul, alas, were to abandon her virginity and receive the seed of this world into herself, then she would also have to accept the manure, which the world throws onto its field.

But I call upon You day and night: come dwell in my soul and close all those places where my enemies can enter. Make the cavern of my soul empty and silent, so that no one from the world will want to enter it.

O my soul, my only concern, be on guard and learn to distinguish between the voices striking your ears. And once you hear the voice of your Lord, abandon your silence and resound with all your strength.

O my soul, cavern of eternity, never permit temporal thieves to enter you and kindle their fire within you. Keep quiet, when they shout to you. Stay still, when they bang on you. And patiently await your Master. For He will truly come.

XLIV

I am descending deep into my heart, to see who is dwelling in it besides me and You, O Eternal God.

And I am filled with fear as I find legions of strangers fighting over portions of my heart. I found as many of them in my heart as time contains human and inhuman souls from the Fall of Adam.

And then I understood why my heart has become weary, and cannot receive either You or me into its chambers, but instead shoves us to the outer perimeter -- pushing the proprietors out to the edge of their property.

Even before I came out of the womb of my mother, the world with its desires was dwelling within me.

I used to pay dearly and too dearly for every flattery of the world. I would always break off a piece of my heart and give it as payment, until eventually I gave my whole heart to the world and the flatteries began to become boresome to me.

Old men complain to me about their years, saying: "Our heart has grown old under the weight of many years."

In truth, old men, your heart has not grown old beneath the weight of many years but beneath the weight of many desires.

And so, when alone I advise my heart: break away from yesterday's day, because it has already broken away from you. All those objects, to which desire bound you yesterday, do not exist today. Some of them have changed, others disease has disfigured, still others have died. Nor do the objects of your desires of tomorrow exist. With its whip, time flogs its flock, and its flock sweats and bleeds beneath the blows. But the objects of today's day are throwing into you, my heart--already brimming with shadows of the dead--new desires, which tomorrow will be even more of the same shadows of the dead.

Do not revive memories of the past, my heart, for these memories will bind you to the pillar of time as many times as you revive them. And you will be a slave to time; you will grow old and will die before death.

As quickly as possible break the knots of the passions, which have become entangled by desires and emotions combining and frequently recurring. It is easier to break the individual threads of desires and the individual threads of emotions than the knots of passions. Nevertheless you must break them even if it causes you to bleed, if you want a new childhood, a new youth, more beautiful and eternal than your former youth.

Cast the world out of yourself, my heart, and then observe how feeble it is. And then observe yourself, and you will feel unheard-of power. The world seems powerful to us only when we serve it as its slave.

You will be as vast as eternity, and eternity itself will come to dwell within you.

O triune God, You have a heart that is devoid of darkness and free of the world. Clear out from my heart the uninvited strangers, who have sullied my heart with darkness. Let my heart be radiant; let darkness hover around my heart, but let it never occupy it.

Let my heart be the heart of a son and a Lord and not the heart of a hireling and a thief.

Grant me the heart of Jesus, around which darkness waited in vain to enter, but never could.

O Queen of heavenly beauty, embrace my heart with motherly caring.

O Holy and Almighty Spirit, make my heart fruitful with heavenly love--so that everything that is born and grows within it may not be of flesh and blood but of Thee, my Holy Spirit and Lord.

XLV

I descend deep into my mind, and I find within it the Jews, who prevent You from entering, my Light-bearing King, and who have filled the whole world with stories about their flight from the kingdom of Pharaoh, a kingdom which has not fled from them.

And after I looked around at everything that was swelling in my mind, I exclaimed: All this is neither myself, nor my God, nor the Kingdom of my God.

All these things are echoes and images of the world, which my overly assiduous senses have brought in from outside and have amassed in my mind.

So where am I? Where is my King and my Lord? Where is the Kingdom of my King? Have you actually dragged the entire realm of Egypt into the promised land? And have you brought all the mud of the Nile into the city of my King?

Wretched is the nourishment of my mind, as long as it is nourished only with what the senses offer it. External vestiges and notions, shadows of shadows, magnified to monstrous proportions (for shadows always grow monstrously huge where there is little light) -- is this in fact my mind? I have discovered that all the cogitation of my mind amounts to nothing more than constructing frail structures out of frail shadows.

Yet again I surveyed the vast field of my mind, where with the speed of many spiders entire cities, more fragile than cobwebs, had been constructed from shadows and demolished --and I became sad, and I reasoned with my inner self:

Where can shadows dance except in light? Is this light not my mind? Would the shadows not gradually grow smaller to the degree that the light of the mind grows stronger? Yet is not even my mind nothing more than a frail shadow of the mind of God?

Alas for me if my mind--after it is separated from the body, which is bequeathing it such an inheritance--is to be left alone in eternity with such a terrifying tapestry!

And in solitude I repeat to my mind: now, while I am seeing nothing, while I am hearing nothing, while I am smelling nothing, while I am tasting nothing, while I am touching nothing -- what is filling you now, if not merely the shadowy images and memories of what you have heard, seen, smelled, tasted and touched? All this has disappeared into the past, has changed, become disfigured, disintegrated, and died. Why do you not bury the dead once and then leave the dead to the dead and flee, instead of standing there like a graveyard, in which the shadows of the dead dance while waiting for new corpses?[34]

How the Jerusalem on high, the city of my King, has transformed itself into a kingdom of the dead and into the trash dump of the world.

O my King, I hear Your mysterious whisper, and I understand; I see Your light, and I comprehend.[35]

And when I understand and comprehend, joy brings tears to my eyes, and I cry: "My salvation is in my Lord!"

He is the light of my mind, for which I have been a sleepy sentry, and as a result strangers have crept in and have darkened the royal light.

My Lord will help me -- once I admit that there is no other helper in all realms -- to expel the darkness and the dark strangers from my mind.

---

[34] "But Jesus said... 'Follow Me, and let the dead bury their own dead.'" (Matt. 8:22).

[35] "Then Jesus spoke to them again, saying, 'I am the light of the world. He who follows Me shall not walk in darkness, but have the light of life.'" (John 8:12).

Let the groom of gloom hover around my mind, but let him not enter into the city of the King of Light.

XLVI

I descend deep into my soul to see who is being born within her and who is departing from her.

How dreadful is the depth of the soul of man, O Bride of Heaven, when a man dares to plunge into her! One who dares to do so plunges through the world and through Hades all the way to the milkwhite choirs of angels, who surround You like Your outer raiment.

I was astonished, when I beheld all the multitudinous offspring of my soul, who were frightened of me and flew off to the side like frightened ravens from carrion.

And my soul was lying there debauched with drunkards of Babylon like a slut, who had forgotten her betrothed.

And with the wrath of a weakling and in the manner of one caught in the act, my soul began to justify herself. Even before there was an accusation she began to justify herself by saying: "Am I not bearing you sons? Am I not sending you spirits?"

But I hid my face for shame and said: Truly, and in this are to be found both my downfall and yours, because you keep bearing me sons when I need the Son, and you keep sending me spirits when I need the Spirit.

You have not borne me sons but hirelings and thieves. You have sent me not spirits but the unclean demons of Hades.

As a virgin you were given to me, your kinsman, for protection, so that you would conceive from the Holy Spirit and bear me the Son. But you, wretched wench, have not conceived from God but from the world, and you have not borne me God but the world.

Why did you not wait for the Spirit of God in virginity, rather than receive the spirits of darkness, who have multiplied within you and have enslaved my heart?

You were raised to be a temple for God, but you have turned yourself into a wayside tavern, where thieves drop in and loll.

Why did you not give birth to the Son of Wisdom, who would have given you light and a good reputation, instead of bearing me sons of evil, who have seized my mind, and have repaid you with darkness and irrationality?

Behold you are being nourished with the same sort of fruit as you have borne. And everything that is coming out of you, is returning to you multiplied.

Oh if you knew, my soul, if you only knew the beauty of the heavenly Virgin, whose image you were supposed to be within me! If you knew how marvelous and mighty the Spirit is, who overshadowed Her![36] If you

---

[36] Cf. Luke 1:35.

only knew how exceedingly handsome and majestic the Son is, whom She bore! I assure you, my ugliness, that you would burst into tears of blood, for you have stamped the seal of your ugliness on my body as well.

And you would cast out the unclean spirits, my soul, and would chase them away into the swine.[37] And you would kick out your offspring, who have been feeding both you and themselves hogwash.

And you would cense your home with the most fragrant incense, and would illuminate it with altar candles. You would adorn it with flowers and stars. And the angels, who surround your Heavenly Lady like milkwhite raiment, would freely come to visit you and would bear the glad tidings of the Annunciation,[38] at which your womb would tremble. Your womb would tremble like the morning dew on the mountain beneath the gentle blows of the sunbeams.

And you would rejoice, my soul, among the prodigal souls of the earth. And you would give birth to the Son, who with His light would drive out the illusory shadows from my mind and who with His fire would consume the worldly desires in my heart. And He would free my entire life from the power of evil spirits, and would wrap it entirely in the mantle of the power and the glory of the Spirit of God.

I see tears instead of anger in your eyes and I am glad, my repentant soul.

---

[37] Cf. Mark 5:11-13.
[38] Cf. Luke 1:26-38.

I observe your silence, in which a rebellion against yourself is being born.

Repent and be restored, my soul, repent while you still have time. Array yourself in virginity quickly; more quickly, before your defiled temporality becomes a defiled eternity.

XLVII

Come closer to me, closer still, O majestic Spirit of Truth. Draw near, and enter into me, more deeply than light and air enter me. Indeed, I can spend an entire night without light, but without You I cannot even lie down on my bed. I can take ten steps without air, but without You I cannot even take one.

Take up your abode in my soul more deeply than my thought can follow. The entire universe is insufficient to encourage my soul to persevere in virginity, if You do not encourage her.

The world incessantly asks for the hand of my soul, in order to be wedded to her. The world offers my soul all its treasures, if only she will abandon her waiting for You. The world whitewashes all its sepulchres,[1] just to entice my soul. The world sets all its ashes out in the sun and pours flattery and pomposity all over it, just to seduce my soul.

Manifest all Your splendor, O Holy Spirit, so that my soul may recognize whose bride she is.

Come closer to me, closer still, O Power of the Holy Trinity. Enter into my consciousness more deeply than thoughts and emblems of the world can. In the same way as a wise mother, when she conceives, prepares and embellishes a cradle for her child, so prepare and embellish my mind for that which will be begotten from You, O Beauty and Purity.

Many evil thoughts lurk like serpents around the cradle of Your Son. And many wicked desires emerge from my heart and seek the cradle of Your Prince, to poison Him with their arrows.

Defend the cradle of my mind, and teach my soul how to give birth and care for an infant.

Shroud in deep darkness the journey of all malevolent visitors coming to see my newborn son. And raise aloft a most radiant star over the way of the Wise Men from the East[2] men who are truly wise, because they are coming to visit my most precious child with three gifts -- faith, hope, and love.[3]

Come closer to me, closer still, O majestic Son of God. Descend deeper into my heart than any emotion, or desire, or passion of the world can descend into it. Protect my heart from the countless merchants, from the numerous buyers and sellers, who are forever swarming in legions around my young and inexperienced heart. And teach my heart not to be crazy about the motley illusions of people and things.

Take up Your abode in the bottom of my heart, as the master of a house does in his own home, my beloved Son, and be for me a merciless judge and a sagacious counselor.

Once purity of soul and sagacity of mind occupy my heart, truly in vain will evil spirits dance attendance in order to step into it.

And my heart will be filled with an ineffable heavenly peace, and will glorify God in chorus with the cherubim and the seraphim. And enriched, it will return to the soul and the mind what it borrowed, for as their equal it will recompense them in equal measure.

And my heart will be filled with sweet love for its Lord, and with compassion for and good will toward suffering souls in the world and in Hades.

Come closer to me, still closer, my majestic Lord.

XLVIII

All the prophets have from the beginning cried out to my soul, imploring her to make herself a virgin and prepare herself to receive the Divine Son into her immaculate womb;

Imploring her to become a ladder, down which God will descend into the world, and up which man will ascend to God;[39]

Imploring her to drain the red sea of sanguinary passions within herself, so that man the slave can cross over to the promised land, the land of freedom.[40]

---

[39] Cf. Gen. 28:12 and John 1:51.
[40] Cf. Ex. 14.

The wise man of China admonishes my soul to be peaceful and still, and to wait for Tao to act within her. Glory be the memory of Lao-tse, the teacher and prophet of his people!

The wise man of India teaches my soul not to be afraid of suffering, but through the arduous and relentless drilling in purification and prayer to elevate herself to the One on high, who will come out to greet her and manifest to her His face and His power. Glorious be the memory of Krishna, the teacher and prophet of his people!

The royal son of India teaches my soul to empty herself completely of every seed and crop of the world, to abandon all the serpentine allurements of frail and shadowy matter, and then--in vacuity, tranquility, purity and bliss--to await nirvana. Blessed be the memory of Buddha, the royal son and inexorable teacher of his people!

The thunderous wise man of Persia tells my soul that there is nothing in the world except light and darkness, and that the soul must break free from the darkness as the day does from the night. For the sons of light are conceived from the light, and the sons of darkness are conceived from darkness. Glorious be the memory of Zoroaster, the great prophet of his people!

The prophet of Israel cries out to my soul: Behold, the virgin will conceive and bear a son, whose name will be -- the God~man.[41] Glorious be the memory of Isaiah, the clairvoyant prophet of my soul!

---

[41] Cf. Is. 7:14.

O heavenly Lord, open the hearing of my soul, lest she become deaf to the counsels of Your messenger.

Do not slay the prophets sent to you[42], my soul, for their graves contain not them, but those who slew them.

Wash and cleanse yourself; become tranquil amid the turbulent sea of the world, and keep within yourself the counsels of the prophets sent to you. Surrender yourself entirely to the One on high and say to the world: "I have nothing for you."

Even the most righteous of the sons of men, who believe in you, are merely feeble shadows which, like the righteous Joseph, walk in your shadow. For mortality begets mortality and not life. Truly I say to you: earthly husbands are mistaken when they say that they give life. They do not give it but ruin it. They push life into the red sea and drown it, and beforehand they wrap it in darkness and make it a diabolical illusion. There is no life, O soul, unless it comes from the Holy Spirit. Nor is there any reality in the world, unless it comes down from heaven.

Do not slay the prophets sent to you, my soul, for killing is only an illusion of shadows. Do not kill, for you can slay no one but yourself.

Be a virgin, my soul, for virginity of the soul is the only semi-reality in a world of shadows. A semi-reality--until God is born within her. Then the soul becomes a full reality.

Be wise, my virgin, and cordially receive the precious gifts of the wise men from the East, intended for your

---

[42] CL Matt. 23:37.

Son. Do not glance back toward the West, where the sun sets, and do not crave gifts that are figmental and false.

XLIX

Conceal my soul from evil eyes, O God, when she gives birth to Your wisdom. Isolate me from people, in a shepherd's cave. Let no one among mortals accompany me except the shadow of one righteous man. In the grotto of Bethlehem, in the cave of stone that has never blasphemed Your name, let my pregnant soul seclude herself here.

Let the innocent lambs and calves keep her company, for from birth they are intended to be food for those who are less pure than they themselves are.

Let the heavenly fires burn silently, and let them fearfully gaze upon a humble corner of the universe, upon the black earth, and upon the most precious part of that corner, upon the grotto that is giving birth to God.

Let earthly kings go far away, and let philosophizing town squabblers not draw near.

The humble herders of lambs and calves will stand around my cave, and will watch as Heaven opens; and they will sing with heavenly angels, when my soul gives birth to my Saviour. Let all others move further away who live by means of fleeting saviors and salvations.

With your light, O Lord, guide the wise men of the East, and the prophets, and the saints to the grotto of my soul, so that they may bring to her the three most precious gifts of mankind from the East.

The first gift is a clairvoyant knowledge of You, which surpasses all other types of knowledge. Let the bearer of this gift cense his precious goods with the prayers of all the prophets of the East and of all the altars of the eastern prophets.

The second gift is the clairvoyant expectation of Your birth in the purity of virginity: let the bearer of this gift keep fasting for the entire journey, lest his eye be confounded by the fat of the earth, and so that he may not lose sight of the guiding star.

The third gift is a clairvoyant love for You. Let the bearer of this gift keep vigil over his gift over the course of his journey, lest his heart stumble over some earthly allurement and be tardy for the adoration of the newborn Infant.

Truly all my mind, and all the consciousness of my mind will accompany one of the three. All my heart, and all the desires of my heart, will accompany another. And my soul, filled with grace and love, will await the third.

Nevertheless the priestly wayfarers will make their journey carefully, making stops along their route to ask the way, which will endanger my soul and the first-born of my soul. As naive as doves, they will ask the way!

But You are infinitely compassionate and infinitely wise. For over fifty centuries You have been amassing precious gifts in the East. And You have not permitted the bearers of these gifts to fall into the hands of thieves.

From before eternity You have been preparing the birth of the Son in the virgin soul. You will not permit Him to be slain by Herod, someone whom the earth bore and crowned in the Egyptianized city of Jerusalem.[43]

Conceal my soul, O God, from the many evil eyes.

L

In the sluggish carriage of the body my Soul journeys through this world of illusions, which are trying to prove their existence by means of their sluggishness and massiveness.

O Light-bearing Lord, how dreadfully and drunkenly stuck to this sluggish carriage my soul has become! In her blindness she thinks that, if she were to fall from this carriage, she would be able to fall down lower still--as though she were not standing on the same ashes whether on the wood or beneath the wood!

In her fear and ignorance my soul has entirely surrendered herself to the body, merely in order for the body to convey her as slowly and sluggishly as possible on the road to a disastrous end.

Her own lordship, her own reality--the only reality in this world-the soul has handed over to the body out of fear and ignorance. She has handed over a mirror to a blind man, and the blind man has shattered it into pieces.

---

[43] Cf. Matt. 2:13-18.

Remember your beginning, O soul, when you were like a sunbeam and the body was like moonlight. Back then you were as piercing and translucent as sunlight, and your carriage was as swift as moonlight.

At that time you used to know that essence was within you, and that your carriage was merely your shadow and something loaned to you. And you knew nothing of fear, for you had your sight and saw yourself borne aloft on the wings of power and immortality.

The sluggish carriage in which you are now riding, is what you yourself wanted of your own free will, according to your own fear and your own ignorance, and you yourself created it.

God did not wish to make you the way you are now, nor your body the way it is now. In order to rid yourself of some slight darkness, into which you were tossed by your desire, you plunged into denser and denser darkness, until you became altogether dark, became heavy, and made a garment for yourself--until you eventually surrendered all your dignity to your corpulent garment, just to rid yourself of fear.

You gave your essence to one who could not bear it, and thus you lost it in both ways; and you became a nonessential and frightful shadow like your body. For essence is a sacred object, and as soon as it is brought out into the bazaar to be bought and sold, it leaves both the buyer and the seller and drifts away from both to an equal extent.

Therefore even the great wise man of India has denied you essence, O soul--to you no less than to your bodily raiment. However, if God descends into you, and is born within you, you will gladden the saddened Hindu sage, who sits in lotus position and meditates, for you will have restored the lost essence. Truly, all essence lies in God, and outside God there is no essence, not even so much as a mustard seed.[44]

Behold, I see within you, my soul, a tiny nook, like a candle-illumined cave in a massive mountain overladen with darkness. The more deeply I peer into the light concealed within you, the more it seems to me to resemble your virginal beauty, your pristine beauty, my soul. Since my peering the dim light has been growing brighter, and more and more clearly one can distinguish in it the wondrous face of a virgin-like a sunbeam arrayed in moonlight.

Here is your salvation, my frightened soul. Here is your life--everything else is a sepulchre. If only you would make this dim light burst into ablaze, and bring this blazing bonfire into my mind and into my heart.

Come to your senses, my soul, and fix your gaze on the little cave where the youthful virgin dwells. Lo, out of this cave deliverance will come to you. Within it even now you will find all your remaining strength, your unblemished beauty, and your unsold immortality.

Outside the cave, outside my soul, where a virgin gives birth to God, everything is shadow and ash, including the sluggish carriage of the body.

---

[44] Cf. Matt. 13:31-32 and 17:20.

LI

O Holy Spirit, behold how vile my soul is! How she fearfully conceals Your fruit within herself, for fear of the Jews, for fear of the countless children of darkness, whom she has multiplied in herself from her marriage with the world.

She has borne innumerable wolves and foxes, and has placed them in her royal chambers, while Your Son has nowhere to rest His head.[45] And they all seek to keep what has been born of the Spirit. Ah, the accomplices of Herod! For they are afraid of might and true light! And those, who have usurped their crowns and placed them bloodstained on their heads, worry about their crowns most of all.

Flee, my soul, flee with the new fruit of your womb, with your only-begotten fruit; flee into Egypt, into a land even more somber than Israel. Behold, the multitudes of slaves that she has produced in herself from the seed of the world are out to hunt down your only Son, and are seeking to kill Him.[46]

The eyes of malefactors are darker than their crowns, however, and in their blindness they fail to distinguish God's infant. Therefore they will slaughter many infants, in order to slay yours.[47]

---

[45] Cf. Luke 9:58.
[46] Cf. Matt. 2:13-15.
[47] Cf. Matt. 2:16-18.

I once saw a frozen shepherd beside a tiny fire. He never took his eyes off the fire, as though he wanted to help it burn with the embers of his eyes. And he sheltered the fire from the cold wind with his hands, and he kept blowing with his breath, so that it would burn more strongly, grow larger, withstand the winds, and warm him.

In this way are the raging winds from my heart threatening to extinguish the divine candle within you, my soul. And in this way are the raging wicked thoughts from my mind spitting on the only light within you, because it is about to bring about their downfall.

Everything that you, my soul, have multiplied in my mind and in my heart, does not consider you a mother but a stepmother, and there is no one among your repulsive progeny, who would place their finger on your burning tongue to cool it.[48] Now for the first time, you have become a mother for you have borne a Son, who is growing up in obedience to you and the Holy Spirit, and in the tender love of parenthood.

Do not burden His head, O bondswoman,[49] with the slavish cares of this world. He must grow in spiritual power, and be in that which is of His Father. Lo, your Son comes like a flame, which will consume your adversaries, and will warm and sanctify you.

As a messenger He comes from a kingdom, where you used to reign in virginal purity and beauty. How can you fail to recognize your Son, my demented soul?

---

[48] Cf. Luke 16:24.
[49] Cf. Gal. 4:21-31.

As a herald He comes from the kingdom of light, where you also used to shine with the splendor of many suns, to summon you into that kingdom once again. How can you not distinguish the voice of your Son, my deaf soul?

As a champion of freedom He comes from a kingdom of freedom, where you also used to dwell, unacquainted with the fear and hunger of slavery, -- He comes to free you from the heavy chains, in which the obesity of the world has shackled you. How can you still hesitate to greet your liberator with cheering, my dumb soul?[50]

O Spirit Almighty, strengthen the salvation-bearing Infant in the cradle of my soul. And protect Him from all the poisoned arrows flying at Him from Israel above and from Egypt below.

LII

Rejoice, my soul your Infant has grown up, and has girded Himself with a strength mightier than the earth. The Demolisher of all your towers of smoke has grown up in the world, and the world has neither noticed nor recognized Him.

The wilderness has been His companion, and meditation and prayer have bound Him to heaven, His homeland.

Behold Him, as He now of His own free will sets out to visit your swarthy offspring. In His eyes eternity glistens; and on His face eternity is written; and in His hands eternity resides. Mightier than the world, behold,

---

[50] Cf. Gal. 5:1.

He goes forth to struggle against the world -- against all your shadowy world, my enslaved soul. Rejoice, my soul, see how your Infant has grown up, undetected by the world, and has girded Himself with a strength mightier than the world.

As calm as any heroic man of mettle, who is conscious of his own invincible might even before his adversaries' vulnerability is vanquished, my Beloved stepped out among the wild beasts, and the beasts cleared out of His way, filled with fright.

In truth, nature recognized Him before people did, and submitted itself to Him as a lawful servant submits himself to his lawful Lord.

But among men only one recognized Him,[51] and he began to cry out, and his cry became the voice of one crying in the wilderness, a voice that men quickly strangled by violence and bloodshed.[52] For violence is the weapon of the weakling, and bloodshed is the way of weakness, from Cain to Herod.

The father of all the tyrants from the beginning of the world[53] greeted Him and offered Him all the treasures of this world, if only He would spare and not trample on his crops in the world.[54]

The ruler of this world saw my Favorite, just as in the morning the shadow of night watches the rising of the sun and dies while watching.

---

[51] John the Baptist (cf. Matt 3.1-17).
[52] Cf. Mark 6:14-29.
[53] Satan (cf. John 8:44).
[54] Cf.Matt 4:1-11.

As the herald of the living and everlasting Trinity, my Favorite stood before the ruler of the world of illusions. And the king of darkness tried to introduce disharmony and confuse the personified trinity in unity. And so, in his customary way, using the craft he had tested on the human race, he first flattered the stomach of my Champion. If he could entrap His stomach first, he would then give it hegemony over the heart and the mind, and would make them shadows and servants of the stomach.

But the lower man remained in unscathed harmony with the middle and upper man. The stomach of my Champion remained faithful to the united trinity, in which the three are coequal and one.

Then the ruler of darkness and evil struck with flatteries at the heart of my Favorite. The heart of the latter, however, being brighter than light, did not receive darkness into itself, but instead remained as faithful as His stomach to His threefold harmony.

Finally the ruler of darkness mustered all his dark powers and attacked the mind of my Saviour, urging Him to test God with nonsensical, breakneck miracles.

The mind of my Only-Begotten, however, was like a blazing torch that scorches every impurity and then puts it to flight. And so not even the mind left the sweet harmony of holy triunity.
Thus did my Victor win the first victory over the king of smoke and ashes, who then came forth to negotiate with my General, offering him everything --except dominion over the world.

LIII

Let heaven descend and let the earth arise, when the pre-eternal Nous, born of the Holy Spirit and the Most Pure Virgin in the cave of my soul, opens His mouth.

His words drip onto cemeteries, and ashes turn green and blossom.

Those rejected by the world, who have also rejected the world, run to greet Him, but those cherished by the world flee from Him in terror.

"I and the Father are one.[55] Before man was, I am."[56]

--Thus speaks Wisdom, born in your virginity, my soul. Listen and understand your eternity, which was lost in the ashes of time.

"Every soul, who does the will of the heavenly Father, can be called a mother of God's Wisdom." [57]

Thus speaks the Wisdom of God, born of the Holy Spirit within you, my soul:

"I am the life and the resurrection of the dead.[58] Whoever severs his bond with Me, has severed his bond with life and becomes like a cloud of smoke in which there is neither light nor moisture.

---

[55] Cf. John 10:30.
[56] Cf. John 8:58 and 17:5.
[57] Cf. Matt. 12:50.
[58] Cf. John 11:25.

"You who think that you are alive, but are in fact a dead cloud of smoke blown about by capricious winds; come to Me, and I shall fill you with light and water, with true light and living water, and you will be truly alive.[59]

"You who are voluntarily coming to Me and filling yourselves with My life, are losing yourselves, such selves as the world made you, and are becoming one with Me, just as I am one with the heavenly Father.[60]

"Truly you will no longer fear time, for time is the scourge of the world, and belongs to the world, not to Me.

"Nor will you be confounded by tribulations in time and space. All tribulations are merely the imaginary hissing of time's scourge in a playground, and they belong to the world, not to Me.[61]

"Peace I give to you, peace which time cannot consume, peace which space cannot constrict, peace which even all the tribulations of the world cannot confound.[62]

"Those who are filled with the world are devoid of life, and are slaves of the world. Those who are filled with life are devoid of the world, and are the sons of life.

"I am full of life, and there is no death in Me, not even so much as the tip of a needle. Therefore the world fails to recognize Me, for there is nothing of the world within Me. The world knows only its own, just as life knows only its own.

---

[59] Cf. Jn. 4:10-14 and 8:12.
[60] Cf. Jn. 17:11, Mt. 10:39; 16:25.
[61] Cf. John 16:33.
[62] Cf. John 14:27 and Phil 4:7.

"And truly, I am the most unknown guest in the world. I have come to offer, not to take. From My own fullness I offer; from nothingness there is nothing to take. My fullness -- is the fullness of God, who sent Me into the world to give Myself to the world, to bring cemeteries to life, and then to return again to the Kingdom of Life. I and life are one. Before Adam was, I am; and after Adam was, I am."[63]

O my soul, rise from the dead! While the One who can resurrect you is within you, arise! If He ever leaves you, you will not be able to do anything except give birth to the dead and bury the dead.

Transform yourselves into listening and obedience, you lifeless offspring of my soul, and arise from the tomb.

LIV

O Son of life, fill the earth of my body and Soul with Your life, so that I may have something with which to appear among the living angels.

Without Your life I would be unable to breathe the air that the angels breathe, or to eat the bread that angels eat. I would again be an exile outside the gates of the heavenly kingdom, before which gates even now I lie like a paralytic.

The world lures me to its bread, and then stones my soul.

---

[63] Cf. Rev. 1:8 and see I AM in the Glossary.

It lures me to a fish, and then stones my heart.

It lures me to light, and then shrouds my mind in darkness.

I do not despise one who is poor, but the world has become despicable to me; because, though it is poor, it pretends to be rich. Neither do I despise one who is selfish, but the world has become despicable to me; because, though it is selfish, it pretends to be generous. Nor do I despise one who is insane, but the world has become despicable to me; because, though it is insane, it pretends to be sane. Nor do I despise one who is sick, but the world has become despicable to me; because, though tuberculous, it intentionally contaminates the water of the healthy. I despise the imposter and the charlatan, O Lord, who bury my life with earth while speaking continuously to me about heaven.

There was once a rich shopkeeper who died. His shop and its goods were bought up by neighbors and his shop stood there empty, but always with the name of the deceased merchant still over the doors, together with lists of all the valuable gifts in the shop.

"I too am like this sort of shop," I say to myself in shame. "I still bear the name of life, but my life is all bought up by my neighbors."

O Son of God, Son of Life, fill my earthliness with life.

First clear the stones from my soul, and nourish it with true bread.[64] Purge my heart of serpents and fill it with Yourself. And dispel the darkness from my mind, and flood it with the light of heaven.

---

[64] Cf. John 6:22-40.

For I shall not truly return to life, if only my soul returns to life while my heart remains stuffed with mortal desires. Nor shall I be resurrected into Your Kingdom, O Lord, if only my heart is purified while my mind still remains filled with darkness.

Truly, until all three fountainheads within me are clarified, my life will be bereft of life. If one is clarified, the other two will muddy it.
If two are clarified, the third is sufficient to muddy them both. Each of the three fountainheads within me is either the contaminator or the saviour of the other two.

O Son of Life, fill my earthliness with life. You are my Wisdom, for in You lies not only divine mentality, but also divine virginity and divine sanctity. For had You not been born out of divine virginity and divine sanctity, You would not have been Wisdom, but finite human knowledge and expertise.

O Son of God, You are the only nourishing bread of my life. I beseech You, do not turn Your face away from me, a sinner. You are the only living water that can water the parched desert of my life.[65]

I beseech You, do not turn Your face away from me, a sinner. You are the only fresh air, that can heal the infirmity of my life.
I beseech You, do not turn Your face away from me, a sinner. But have mercy on me and save me!

---

[65] Cf. John 7:38.

LV

"Who are You?" the children of the world ask the Son, O my virgin soul.

For they see Him walking among them as a King among slaves. And they listen to His powerful words, but fail to understand. And they behold His powerful deeds, and are filled with fear. And they feel power going out of Him, and are confounded.

But your Son--the fairest among the sons of men, with the clear eyes of an ox, with the peacefulness of a lamb, with the strength of a lion, with the soaring loftiness of an eagle, and with the face of an angel--answers them: "I am the Truth. I have come from the Truth, I bear you a gift from the Truth, and I am returning to the Truth.[66]

"If truth were in you, you would have recognized Me and would not have asked: 'Who are you?'

"Truly, you do not even know how to ask who you are; how then will you understand if I tell you -- who I am?

"Lo, you are nothing by yourselves alone. You are like a dream separated from the dreamer. You are neither two seconds in time nor two paces in space. As when

---

[66] In the vision of Ezekiel, the prophet saw four winged creatures in a whirlwind. Each of the four had the face of a man, a lion, an ox, and an eagle (cf. Ezek. 1:10). In patristic writings and Christian iconography, these symbolize the four evangelists; i.e., the angel of St. Matthew, the lion of St. Mark, the ox of St. Luke, and the eagle of St. John. The "lamb" would symbolize Christ as "the Lamb of God" (cf. John 1:29 and Rev. 4:7 and 5:6).

smoke drifts over the lake and its shadow dances on the water, so is your life also an empty and non-existent dancing of shadows.

"Only you still have not forgotten how to utter the word 'truth,' but this is all that remains to you of the Truth. You call the glitter of matter truth, as though you were a lifelong captive in a dungeon who had only heard of the sun, and called an insect--a firefly--the sun.

"When someone comes to know the Truth, Truth takes up its abode in him. He becomes one with the Truth and is no longer half a man but a whole man. Truth heals him and makes him whole, while illusion chops a man up into pieces and grinds him into powder.

"Just as it is no longer possible for the scattered ashes of a tree to recognize a verdant tree, so is it impossible for you to recognize Me.

"Truly I am the Truth, the same yesterday, today, and tomorrow.[67] The Spirit of Truth, who is with Me, He it is who also speaks through Me and He it is who lives within Me. Without Him I would be nothing, just as you yourselves are. But because of Him living within Me, I am the One Who Is.

"I have come down from on high, like frightful rain, to fill a parched river bed, which you always used to call a river.

---

[67] Cf. John 14:6 and Heb. 13:8. In Serbian, the words for "truth" (istina) and "the same" (isti) share a common stem.

"Others brought laws, but I bring the Truth.[68] Others cleared the river bed of its dried mud and prepared it for water, but they could not supply the water. I am supplying the water; I am filling the river bed; and I am justifying the river's name.

"I have not come to your drought-stricken land to teach you how to dig for ground water; rather I-- the Living Water--have come so that thirsty souls may drink Me.[69]

"Neither have I come to teach you how to make bread, but rather to be bread for all souls that hunger.[70]

"Neither have I come down into your darkness to teach you how light is created, but rather to illumine you. Indeed, even the sun--a light far dimmer than Myself-- does not teach how light is emitted, but instead illumines.

"Neither have I descended into this maniacal quivering of shadows to teach you what reality is, but rather to be Reality, in regions of emptiness and nothingness.

"Truly, I have not come to you as a teacher of wisdom, but as Wisdom itself.

"Whoever does not accept Me, does not eat Me, does not drink Me, does not breathe Me, and thereby does not become one with Me, remains outside Me --which means he remains outside of Life and Truth."

---

[68] "For the law was given through Moses, but grace and truth came through Jesus Christ." (John 1:17).
[69] Cf. John 7:38.
[70] Cf John 6:22-59.

LVI

My soul runs after truth, O Son of Truth, and there is no end to her running and no term adequate to describe her exhaustion.

It would be better to be at peace, my soul, and to attract truth to yourself by means of your peace. What would you think of someone who said at midnight: "I cannot bear to be without light, I must run to the sun to bring back some rays?"

Why begin a race of a thousand years, when light is faster than you and can fall into your lap in a matter of seconds?

Open yourself to light, O soul, and light will come into you.

The walls that stand between you and truth and loom up before you like colossal mountains, which you have been trying to cross by running to the point of exhaustion, are your own creation and are more fragile than the white foam on the lake. If only you could open your eyes wide enough *not* to see them. Truly, the existence of these walls depends upon your seeing them. If you did not wish to see them, they would not exist.

I once watched a chicken on top of a blackboard running around inside a circle that had been drawn on it with white chalk. I watched him for a long time as he ran to and fro and hesitated to jump over the white line, which he probably perceived to be a living creature or a high wall.

This is like my soul, I said in sorrow, when she thinks that she is cut off from her freedom either by some mighty giants or by frightful towering walls. In actual fact, between her prison and her freedom there exists only an imaginary line, thinner than a hair.

All the walls of your prison, my soul, consist of your fear of the world, of your desire for the world and of your thoughts about the world. All these walls you yourself have built according to the instructions of your senses from the material that they have given you, a material that is truly more fragile than foam.

In the beginning you did not have senses, my soul, and you were not separated from truth. After you became blind, you sent out your senses to chase after truth. And those greyhounds have been chasing and fetching the closest and easiest game, and bringing back wolves to their blind master, who has been eating them as though they were venison.

Do not run, my soul, for it is characteristic of the senses to run. Servants and slaves run, but a master remains peacefully still.

Behold, in that corner of profound peace and virginal purity left within you, your pre-eternal eye has opened. This eye does not see the walls of your prison, therefore neither does it run up mountains that do not exist. This eye is the Son of Truth, one of the Trinity that rules over all the heavenly kingdom, from which you barred yourself by wanting to be the "Fourth." Truly I tell you, a "fourth" does not exist anywhere throughout what exists. His name is -- Nonexistent.

By your playing and clowning around with me in the darkness, my soul, you have made me into a "fourth." All your people out of the world of "fourths" will cast stones at the Son of Truth. Flee, wretched soul, flee from the world of "fourths." Totally unshackle yourself from it, totally reject it, totally despise it and--bow down before the Truth of the Trinity, which is given to you through the Son of Truth.

O Lord of Truth and Life, help my soul to prostrate herself before You and sob: "You are my Being, my Life and my Truth, O beloved Son of the Holy Trinity. You are my everything, and I surrender myself, naked and poor, to You. I no longer have anything to reject or to scorn or to despise, because nothing even exists except You. Have mercy on me, and receive me into Your arms' embrace."

LVII

"Are You the One who is to come?" the sons of earth ask the One born of your Virgin, O my soul.

But the One born of the Virgin glistens with matinal light amid the sons of earth, who are as dark as extinguished days.

The flaming Seraphim shine in His eyes; the sapient Cherubim sit upon His lips; the Lordly Thrones bolster His stance. Seeing Him alone, a Leader without an earthly army, every sane man is convinced that this could be a leader of an awesome and enormous army of invisible powers.

And behold, surrounded by the angelic hosts your Leader, O soul, opens His mouth and speaks:

"In truth, I am the One for whom you have been waiting; do not hope for another. If you have been searching for the way, I am the Way.[71]

"I am your Tomorrow from today until the end of time. Everything good, that you have been expecting from the days of tomorrow, is within Me. Today your tomorrow is fulfilled in Me. And no day, from now until the last day, will bring you what I am bringing you. Lo, I am the day that has no beginning and no end.[72]

"I am the treasury of every future that exists and I am the way to that treasury. The future in its entirety cannot give you so much as a.kernel of good, unless it borrows it from Me.

"All the prophets have pointed out the way that leads to Me. All the ways of the prophets come to an end and lose themselves in Me. From this time forth I am the only Way, and outside Me are only regions without roads or ways. Like many streams flowing into a single river and then losing their way, so have all the prophets flowed into Me, and from this time forth I direct the course of Life. Whoever continues to follow the ways of the prophets further, will be following paths that no longer exist and will injure themselves.

"The prophets came to show the way; I have come to be the Way.

---

[71] Cf. John 14:6.
[72] Cf. Rev. 1:8.

"Whoever wishes to follow Me, must follow Me not with his feet alone, but with all his soul, with all his heart, and with all his mind.[73]

"My way is long, and whoever trusts solely in his feet will drop from exhaustion.

"When children want to keep up with giants, they must forego walking on their own feet and sit on the shoulders of giants.

"Whoever wants to keep up with Me, must renounce his feet, his soul, his heart, and his mind. Whoever renounces all this, I shall take onto My feet, into My soul, into My heart, and into My mind. And he will not be heavy for Me, nor shall I be tiring for him. However, anyone who fails to renounce everything, cannot overtake or detain Me along the way.[74]

"I am the Way, and he who follows My Way, does not journey alone but with Me. The prophets used to point out the way hither or thither or over in that direction, because they were not themselves the way. I cannot point out the way: hither, thither, or over in that direction; nor can I leave any of my wayfarers to journey without Me. Whoever wishes to follow My Way, I Myself shall carry.[75]

"I tell you one thing more: I am what is desired tomorrow and the Way to tomorrow. Without Me you cannot find the way to what you desire tomorrow, nor can you expect it."

---

[73] Cf. Matt. 22:37.
[74] Cf. Matt. 16:24.
[75] Cf. Matt. 11:29-30.

O God-bearing Son, have mercy on us and begin leading us Yourself.

LVIII

Do you ask me for the way, exhausted runners?

To what are you racing, sons of men? If you knew what you were jogging toward, you would also know the way.

Your destinations are innumerable, therefore your ways are also innumerable.

You collide with one another and curse at each other, because your pathways cut across each other.

Even if there were as many of you as there are blades of grass on the earth, you would not be colliding with one another, if you had one destination and one direction. And your mouths would quit cursing.

Those who search for life and truth, have one destination and one direction. Their destination shows them the way, just as the sun does with light. Truly whoever hides from the sun will lose both his destination and his way, and in vain will he toss himself hither and thither in the dark.

Do not set out in the ways of your thoughts, for they lead you one thought to the next, and they know of no destination or way outside themselves.

Do not set out in the ways of your imaginations, for they allure you to level river beds until they suddenly plunge into an abyss beneath the earth.

Do not trust your soul as long as she tells you that the flesh in which she is clothed is your destination and way. Has clothing ever guided anyone?

The way to the kingdom of blessedness is not found, is not shown, and is not intersected. It is born in the soul when Life and Truth are born in her. If Life and Truth have been born in your soul, rejoice and be glad, for the Way has been born in it as well.[76]

Just as Life cannot be separated from Truth, so the Way cannot be separated from Life and Truth.

Until all three manifest themselves, none has been manifested.

Do not place your hope in tomorrow's day to cast bright light on your erring way. For tomorrow's day is only a new aberration of your way, and a new enigma.

Do not place your hope in days, for days are the garden of your imagination. Instead set all your hope in that Day which is never somber at dawn.

O Lord, my Lord, my triradiate Godhead, who will suffice except You?
The ways of men are a trap, in which runners run all day and at dusk find themselves in the same place. The entrapped ways of men bewilder me and I ask myself: who will suffice for a haven except my Lord?

---

[76] "I am the way, the truth, and the life" (John 14:6).

"Whoever recognizes Me as the destination of his wayfaring," says the Lord, "will have Me as the Way to My mansions."[77]

O Lord, my Lord, my triradiate Godhead, who will dare to enter into Your light?

"Whoever draws near to gaze upon My light within himself, will dare to enter into My light, and will not be scorched."

O soul, my soul, my tri nocturnal darkness, when will you remove your mask and be transfigured into triradiate daylight?

Save yourself while the divine torch is burning above you. For when it goes away from you it will vanish, even as the dancing moonlight has vanished in the depths of the lake.

LIX

How many, many times, my soul, you have sobbed for someone who knew the way, had seen the truth, and possessed life.

You thirstily used to entrust yourself to many expert runners, who would lead you along every way to a certain point, and would then take you back.

You used to listen to many who told tales about the truth, my soul. But when you would pose certain questions to them, questions which burned deep within

---

[77] Cf. John 14:2.

you, their words would get stuck in their throats. And saddened, you would go to other story-tellers, and would hear the same tale over again --a tale which, like all the others, only went so far, like a stretched rubber band.

And those who used to try to explain life to you, would only succeed in opening your eyes to death.

But behold, the One who resurrects is coming, and all-terrifying death flees in terror before Him. Here is a story for you about Life, one which death does not shorten, but lengthens.[78]

Here is a story for you about Truth, one which provides answers to all your guestions before you even pose them.

Here is the Guide for you, whose Way never ends; and once He begins to guide you, He does not go back.

Here is the Good Shepherd,[79] who values the life of one sheep above all the Sabbaths of the Jews.[80] And here is the Healer, to whom the life of a penitent sinner is more valuable than Solomon's temple.[81]

Do not worry, my soul, about any of the sheep in your sheepfold -- not one of them will perish. Neither need you fret over the wolves around the sheep -- not one of them will escape. For your Shepherd has a sharp two-edged sword.

---

[78] Cf. Luke 7:11-17, Mark 5:21-24, 34-43, and John 11:1-44.
[79] Cf. John 10:1-30.
[80] Cf. Luke 15:3-7.
[81] Cf. John 9.

All the sheep are within you, and all the wolves are within you -- the progeny of your marriage with heaven and earth --and behold, my Favorite is coming in with a sharp two-edged sword.

Do not wail, if He hurts you with His sword. He is the Good Physician and He cuts out of you only that which is not you. Do not wail for the strangers who brought you disease, and shame, and grievous wounds. Do not be afraid of the in-extinguishable fire, that He brings into you. For a long time the junk accumulated within you has been in need of a bonfire. The bonfire will last a long time, because the old junk within you has rotted.

The pain that you feel is not your own, my soul, but is the pain of your other marriage and its -- illegitimate children.

Do not lament, if He separates you from a father and a mother, and brothers and sisters.[82] He will not separate you from anything that is of heaven. He would not even consider cutting a single heavenly bond. Indeed, He is only separating and purifying you from earth, and is cutting your bonds with earth.

If you were a chaste virgin, my soul, and saw with the unconfounded eye of celestial innocence, even you yourself would easily break these bonds, for you would see that in truth they do not even exist.

Hurry, my soul, and unite yourself with the Son of the Living God, for He is not waiting for me. Once you unite yourself with Him, behold, neither His sword nor His fire will be frightening to you, but will be as sweet as honey.

---

[82] Cf. Gen. 12:1, Matt. 10:37 and 19:29.

LX

The snows melt on the mountain when the sun shines, and the streams flow to cleanse the earth. What sun will melt the snow from the summits of your souls, O sons of men, and cleanse your earthliness?

Sin has made your souls as stiff as icy frost. Like last year's snow, upon which new snow falls, so does your sin of last year and the years before lie dead-still, providing a bed for the sin of today and tomorrow.

You would have no sins, if you had no sinfulness; if you did not have sinful souls, you would have no sins. Snow would not be able to remain on the mountain, if the earth were warm; if the earth were warm and if the cold fog that hides the sun were to dissipate, the snow would be unable to remain either on the mountain or in the valley.

The cold ground and the cold fog are piling up snow upon snow and ice upon ice between you and your sun.

Who will absolve your sins, and who will thaw your icy hatefulness?

In vain do you yourselves forgive your own sins. By forgiving your own sins you make ice out of the snow, providing an even smoother bed for new snow.
The light of the triradiate Godhead alone can absolve your sins, just as the sun alone can melt the snow on the mountain, thaw the snow and ice, and bring forth flowers out of the black earth.

"Your sins are forgiven you, arise!"[83] Do you know, O man, the One who has the authority to restore your health with these sweet words? I assure you that you will not find or meet Him on earth, even if you were to scour the entire world.

Even if you were to scour all the planets that orbit around the sun, you would not find Him. For He is not from earth, and the earth does not sustain Him.[84]

He is the Celestial Man and the Saviour of your soul. He is far away from anyone who forgives himself his own sins, but He is near, very near to anyone who despises his sins and cries out to heaven to blot them out.

His mind is purer than sunlight, and His word is more searing than the sun. He melts the snow off the soul of man and induces flowers to grow. All those thick layers of snow and ice can be melted by Him, and all the earth can be cleansed by Him. Call upon Him from the depths of your soul, and He will come.

When He exclaims: "Your sins are forgiven" -- your soul, now benumbed by the burden of sins, will become nimble and mobile, and the paralysis of the body will vanish.

The sins of the soul are the wounds of the soul. How can the body be healthy with a wounded soul?

A madman says: "Look at my neighbor, an inveterate sinner, and see how his body blossoms with good health! Surely the sin of the soul does not harm the body," says one who is out of his mind.

---

[83] Cf. Matt. 9:2-8.
[84] Cf. John 8:23.

Just wait, madman, just wait a little longer, until the dung of the soul emerges from the body. Then you will shut your mouth and flee from sins as though you were fleeing fetid putridity. Wait until a worm devours the inside of an apple, and you will be distressed to see its outside all faded and pale.

Then you too will stand with the lepers along the road and cry out like a man near death: "O Son of God, have mercy on me!"[85]

And then you will hear -- and understand those salvationbearing words: "Your sins are forgiven; go in peace!"

LXI

I hear a voice from the depths saying: a sinless man will walk among the sick and will not become sick. For sinfulness is health and strength, the fullness of health and strength.

One who is sinless does not die. And if a sinless man dies on account of the sins of others, he will return to life. Like all diseases -- death too is a disease that sin causes. And just as no disease has power over one who is sinless, so neither does death have any power over him. Truly, sons of earth, even death is nothing more than a disease.

---

[85] Cf. Luke 17:12-19.

Let one who is master over sin arise, and he will be master over sickness as well, and he will heal the sick and resurrect the dead.

Indeed, sinlessness means an abundance of life, but sinfulness -- a dearth of life. Toss red-hot embers onto green grass, and they will not start a fire. But grass desiccated of its life juice will catch fire from the same red-hot embers. Sickness is even more powerless against one who is sinless than fire is to green grass.

One who is sinless has an abundance of life, and gives it;[86] one who is sinful has a dearth of life, and steals it. Whoever has an abundance of life, to him still more is given. Whoever has a dearth of life, from him it is taken away. And the more of it he steals, the less of it he will have. Truly, life is a gift and is only to be given, and through perpetual giving it is multiplied. But one who steals it will shrivel more and more, until he pines away into nothingness.[87]

Over the mountain grass a whisper wanders: sin and sickness can neither devour nor consume life; they can only usurp and take the place of life.

Over the emerald lake a murmur ripples: an abundance of life is stronger than an abundance of sins; and abundance of life both drives out sin and takes the place of sin.

Wandering everywhere all over the earth, a whisper walks: life and sickness relate to one another the way

---

[86] "I have come that they may have life, and that they may have it more abundantly" (John 10:10).
[87] Cf. Matt. 25:29.

existence and nonexistence do; the realm of the one knows nothing of the realm of the other.

Rustling everywhere throughout the starry universe, a murmur rustles: connection with God purges one of sin; connection with God cures one of sickness; connection with God delivers one from death.

The prophets and wise men exclaim what the angels whisper: whoever is connected to life, will live; whoever is connected to death, will die. Whoever knows life, life likewise knows; whoever knows death, death likewise knows. Life has no eyes for death, nor does death have eyes for life.

Behold, how the presence of the One who came down from heaven heals those who have confessed Life, and bow it deadens those, who have confessed death!

Behold, how the Son of the Virgin is brimming with Life, and how He bestows it on those sons of women, who have reverted to virginal modesty and have begun to beseech life of the Giver of Life!

Behold, how easy it is for the Brimming One to pour out, for the Sinless One to absolve sins, for the Healthful One to heal, and for the Life-bearing One to resurrect the dead!
O my soul, arise and walk. Behold, your sins are forgiven. Behold, you are healed of your infirmity, and death is about to flee.

In that tiny portion of territory, which your sin and sickness have not yet seized, stand tall, my soul. And all your former territory, stolen by nonexistence, will be yours once more.

O dear and most gracious Lord, I believe and I confess that You are life.

Just absolve my sins, my Glory, and all the rest will be given to me by You Yourself.

LXII

Warriors of Life, wage war mightily and do not waver in your faith in victory.

Victory is bestowed on the one whose eye keeps its untiring gaze fixed upon it. Whoever even thinks of defeat, loses sight of victory and does not find it again. Victory is a tiny star in the distance, which continuous gazing magnifies and draws nearer!

Keep watch with vigilance, so that not even one of the enemy jumps over the wall into your city. If even one adversary jumps in, the city is lost. Only a single serpent slithered into Paradise, and Paradise was transformed into Hell.[88]

Indeed, just one drop of poison enters a full body of blood, and physicians predict death!

It is not as important to slay your enemy outside the city as it is not to let him into the city.

Warriors of Life, wage war mightily and do not waver in your faith in victory.

---

[88] Cf. Gen. 3.

What does it profit you, if you conquer and gain possession of the world, and the world takes the place of your soul.[89] Truly, the world will remain, but the soul will no longer be yours. The soul is a timid bird; if you throw even a tiny bit of ashes at her, she takes to flight and flees to escape.

The soul is more valuable than the world -- you would do better, therefore, to subjugate the soul rather than the world. The soul is a more faithful ally than the world -- you would do better, to forge an alliance with the soul. The soul is richer than the world -- you would do better, to make her your fortress. The soul is more healthful than the world -- you would do better, to seek your health in her. The soul is more beautiful than the world -- you would do better, to take her for your bride. The soul is a more fruitful field than the world -- you would do better, to exert yourself over her.

Warriors of Life, wage war mightily, and do not waver in your faith in victory.

Do not cast out a demon with a demon. For you will always have a demon in the house. But cast out the devil with God. And the devil will flee, but God will remain.[90]

Do not fight fire with fire. For you will make the fire into a conflagration, and your house will burn down along with your enemy's. But fight fire with water, and you will extinguish it.

Do not raise death as a weapon against death, for you will only increase the range of death. But raise life as a

---

[89] Cf. Matt. 16:26.
[90] Cf. Matt. 12:22-28.

weapon against death, and death will retreat as a shadow does before the face of the sun.

Warriors of Life, wage war mightily, and do not waver in your faith in victory.

Your objective is your weaponry. If you wage war for Life, expect also a crown of glory from Life.

Have neither two objectives, nor twofold weaponry. When the objective is life, life is also the weaponry. When the objective is death, death is also the weaponry. Wherever life and death are intermingled, death is the victor.

Do not expect a reward from both sides. For the other side is death.

Do not serve two masters.[91] For the name of the other master is death.

Sacrifice everything for Life, and expect everything from Life. And Life will give you everything.

Whoever captures Life, has truly taken the wealthiest city in all realms. And he will find more treasure in that city than an eye can behold, a heart can desire, and a dream can dream of.

Warriors of Life, wage war mightily, and do not waver in your faith in victory.

---

[91] Cf. Matt. 6:24.

LXIII

Who brought sin into the world, O Lord, and made the whole world sick, and became nourishment for death?

The mind is the gate, through which sin entered in. Through the mind the drop of poison dripped into the heart and the soul.

Separated from virginity and light, no longer threefold but one-dimensional, the mind separated itself from the holy Triad, and stands as "the fourth" -- nonexistence. It thinks what is mundane, and not what is divine.

Separated from the virginity of the soul and the light of the heart, the mind is the shadow of the Son of God and the reverse of Wisdom. This dark shadow spreads its darkness into the soul and the heart. And once all three have become shrouded in darkness and covered with mildew, it then educates itself into a sort of unholy triad, a shadow of the Holy Triad, just as nonexistence is a quivering shadow of existence.

What is the first sin of the mind, O Lord, by which it introduced pain and suffering into the whole human race?

The first sin of the mind is self-delusion, the second is pride. Riveted to senses intended for nonexistence, the mind accepted nonexistence as existence.

Self-delusion looks at the reflection of the moon in the lake as though it were the actual moon, and rushes to grab it in the water.

Self-delusion sees a rope and mistakes it for a snake, and flees from it.
The self-delusion of a dog sees a dog in the water, and impels the actual dog into barking at his own shadow.

Self-delusion concerning the capricious ashes of this world impels the mind to attach its essence to this world, and blindfolds it with forgetfulness of the truly existent world.

In truth, self-delusion of the mind is the first sin This first sin enters into marriage with pride and out of this marriage are born all the sins and all the evils that produce pain and suffering.

How is it that pride appears immediately after self-delusion, my Lord?
Discoverers of what is new and previously unknown are always filled with pride.

The self-deluded mind keeps discovering for itself something new and previously unknown.

Alas, if the mind only knew that it is discovering its own grave!

The self-delusion of the mind is discovering the nonexistent world as though it were the existent world. Alas, how this "discovering" is becoming such perilous covering! By revealing the nonexistent world to the mind as though it were the existent one, self-delusion is concealing the existent world and representing it to the mind as though it were nonexistent.

O my Lord, the only One who exists, save my mind from these two infernal sins.

My Truth, save me from the pernicious self-delusion of my mind.

O Master and Bestower of all that I am and I have, deliver me from pride, the destroyer of the deranged and the foolish.

LXIV

How marvelous is the true Son of God! The One who is not of shadow but of light. The One who represents the existent Triad and not the nonexistent triad.

How He has supported His wisdom with blessed virginity and powerful light, like the dome of a church with walls of marble!

The Dominions, Powers, and Authorities never take their eyes off Him. The Principalities, Archangels and Angels are His servants.

Like the milk and honey that flow in the Promised Land,[92] so wisdom flows from His lips.

"Where your treasure is, there your heart will be also.[93] I do not ask you what you have but what you are. If you are children of light to such a degree that there is no darkness in any member of your body, then your possession is the Father of Light.

---

[92] Cf. Ex. 3:8.
[93] Matt. 6:21.

"Blessed are you in your treasure, if everything you possess is in the Father of Light. I say to you, even your essence will be in Him. You who have extensive holdings in earthly real estate, beware, lest you become the property of your own real estate.

"Beware lest that which you have been from the beginning becomes that which you have possessed since yesterday. Truly I tell you, you will become slaves of darkness and light will forget you.

"Possessions and close relatives are your enemies. They tie you to this world, and they close the gates of heaven to you.

"Do not bury your heart in earthly property, for beneath the earth it will decay. Offer up your heart to God -- as a gift to the Gift-Giver, and your possessions will become your harmless slave instead of your harmful master.

"Do not give your whole heart to relatives, for they will devour it -- and will remain hungry.

"Instead give your whole heart to the Holy Spirit, and He will nourish your relatives with richer nourishment. In this way your relatives will be related to you, not only because flesh and blood bind you, but because the Holy Spirit binds you. And the Spirit has no bonds except everlasting ones."

O my penitent soul, choose! Do you prefer to exist or to possess? If you prefer to exist, your possessions will amount to no less than God. If you prefer to possess, your existence will be no greater than the moonlight in the depths of the lake.

O Son of God, help my soul not to err and not to choose destruction.

LXV

Where do unclean spirits come from, Most Pure Mother of God?

"From an unclean woman; from her unclean marriage with her own son. The unclean mind defiles the soul, his mother, and out of the unclean soul come forth the unclean spirits, whose main fortress is the heart.

"From their main fortress, the unclean spirits thereupon make assaults on their parents with unclean passion, and they become multiplied both in the soul and in the mind."

How numerous are the unclean spirits, Most Pure Mother of God?

"There are more, far more unclean spirits than clean ones. For they are as weak as a shadow compared to clean spirits. And they gang up in legions against one clean spirit, against a single virginal spirit.

"They multiply most copiously in what is corrupted and they assault most violently what is virgin -- attacking everything that represents chastity in body or in soul, in the male or the female, in the mind or in the heart.

"However many sinful desires as there are in the heart --however many poisonous passions, feelings of fear and feelings of hatred toward everything heavenly as there are -- there are just as many unclean spirits in the heart.

'To whatever extent self-delusion about the world is present in the mind -- whether in ideas and concepts, or in imaginations and words -- unclean spirits are to the same extent present in the mind.

"Moreover all the unclean spirits from the heart sow their seed in the mind. And all the unclean spirits from the mind sow their seed in the heart. And all together, from both the one fortress and the other, they sow their unclean seed in the field of the will. And in the soul, their greatest fortress, there are as many of them as there are shadows in the world.

"And they multiply from each other haphazardly and illicitly, since they are the accursed enemies of any law and order. They view their might and potential victory from the standpoint of quantity rather than quality. They are truly as fragmented as sand, and continue to fragmentize themselves more and more.

"They are multiplied not out of mutual love but out of hellish selfishness. Nor do they sense any bliss whatsoever from their existence. All their time is taken up with fighting over prerogatives and preeminence. Alas for the man, who becomes their battlefield."

What results from unclean spirits operating in man, Most Pure Mother of God?

"Sickness is produced within the inner man and, eventually, in the outer man as well. Sin is the seed of sickness. The seed of sin grows as wildly as weeds.

"All infirmities are the heir of sin. Truly, not only blindness and deafness and dumbness, but all the others as well. And however strange it may seem to say -- death is also a disease, an inheritor of the same cause, a corruption from the same worm."

O Most Pure and Light-bearing Mother of God, set us free from unclean spirits; cleanse us from every sin; heal us from every infirmity, through the mercy of Your Son and the power of Your Holy Spirit.

From the midst of corruption we fall down on our knees and cry out to You: "With Your radiance, O Mother of God, burn up all the corruption that is suffocating us.

LXVI

I entreat you, Seraphim, who first sensed the presence of the Virgin Son in the world?

"The unclean spirits were the first to sense His presence, and were filled with fear. Wherever there is fear, there is also servility; wherever there is servility, there is also impudence. Truly, the worst culprits always have the greatest fear of the judge, and when the judge approaches, they are the first to recognize him.

"The righteous man does not recognize the judge, because he is not thinking about him, nor is he waiting for him. Sin does not induce him to prick up his ears and look to see from which side of the courtroom the judge will appear."

I entreat you, Cherubim, how did the unclean spirits perceive the presence of the Virgin Son in the world?

"In the same way as darkness senses light. What is more sensitive to light than darkness? Still sleeping before dawn, neither mineral, nor vegetable nor animal has any inkling of day, before darkness has already sensed the coming of its devourer, and with trepidation prepares to flee.

"Thus the demons also sensed the coming of the Virgin Son before all the people of earth who were cleaner than they themselves."

I entreat you, Thrones, how did the Virgin Son subjugate the unclean spirits?

"Only to the earth do the unclean spirits simulate some sort of power. Heaven looks upon them as being already subjugated by their own wickedness. When the master of the house shows up on his own property, burglars flee to the fence and search for an opening to escape."

I entreat you, Dominions and Powers, what are the four victories which the Virgin Son won in the world?

"The four victories are the four victories over the four evils, which flow out of each other as a muddy river from a muddy spring.

"The first victory is over the unclean spirits, from which came sin.

"The second victory is over sin, from which came infirmity.

"The third victory is over infirmities, which end with death.

"The fourth victory is over death."

I entreat you, Authorities and Principalities, what is the greatest victory of the Virgin Son?

"None is greater and none is lesser. There is only a victory that is both first and final. The second victory could not have occurred without the first, nor was the third possible without the first and second, nor the fourth without the first, second, and third.

"All four represent one four-fold victory, which illuminates the east, west, north and south of the whole existent world."

I beseech you, Authorities and Principalities, what is the greatest victory of the Son, the celebrated victory of the Virgin Son?

"He who is able to comprehend this celebrated victory, senses it and embraces it.

"Whoever comprehends it, bows down before the Virgin Son day and night.

"Whoever senses it, weeps -- for joy, because he has perceived it, and for shame, because he perceived it so late.

"Whoever embraces it, loses the wedded son within himself, and becomes even himself a virgin son."

To you I fall down and pray, O ranks of saints and martyrs, who have understood, and sensed, and embraced the victory of the Virgin Son. Pray, together with all the angelic hosts, to the Virgin Son for us, who still stand on the field of battle.

LXVII

The earth is a stepmother, O Heavenly Mother, and behaves toward us as a stepmother. She looks upon us as stepchildren, as strangers from afar, as adopted children -- until she makes us her slaves.

We labor for her day and night, and for this she pays us wages with her miserable possessions: sin, sickness, and death.

Whoever only lives by her bread, will never know satiety.[94] Rather, the more he eats, the hungrier he feels. And the more he dances to her tune, the more he will be overcome by grief.[95]

He is like a beast that falls into a deep pit and then digs ever lower and deeper in the earth in order to save himself. And even as he moves further away from salvation, he thinks that salvation is near. Truly, such are the sons of men, who toil hard over the earth, and assess the nearness of salvation on the basis of their toiling.

To what avail is your swimming in ashes, ever deeper and deeper? O sons of men, your salvation has been left behind you.

You say: "We need dig just a little bit deeper, and we shall come out into the light." But I say: "Just a little

---

[94] "Man shall not live by bread alone, but by every word that proceeds from the mouth of God" (Matt. 4:4).
[95] CL Luke 7:32.

deeper into the earth, and you will be further from the light."

You say: "We need only complete certain tasks tomorrow and the day after, and the kingdom of goods will be constructed." But I tell you: "All that you have constructed of earth, will crash down upon your head, and your tomorrow and day-after-tomorrow will again be only a painful lifting of your head beneath the ruins."[96]

Your fathers used to mutter the same words of consolation to themselves, and they died off amid the ruins and amid the unfinished repairs.

You need ladders, and nothing other than ladders; so that you can climb out of the hole into which you have fallen, so that you can flee from the cold embrace of your stepmother.

A virgin is that ladder.[97] She lights a heavenly candle in the midst of your darkness and shows the way. She is clairvoyant, and she knows that which you have forgotten. Alienated from earth, she has been befriended by heaven. Disrobed of darkness, she is clothed in light. Through her Heaven peers into us. Through her we can see heaven.

She is cautious with regard to your counsels; rectitude is in her mouth; heavenly wisdom is in her womb; a reverend flame is in her heart.

Out of her come the healer and the cure. From her thighs come the guide and the way.

---

[96] Cf. Luke 20:17-18.
[97] Cf. Gen. 28:12.

She is not a stepmother but a mother, and does not promise her son more than she can give. Her giving is her promise, while the giving of the stepmother consists of promises.

The stepmother is earth, O Heavenly Mother, and she behaves toward us as a stepmother. With a black veil she conceals You from our eyes, so that we may not see You and think that You are dead. Therefore generation after generation snuggles up to the stepmother, and kisses her harsh hand.

Flash Your face, O Mother, and the stepmother will flee, and the slaves will become sons.[98]

LXVIII

The Hindu curses karma The Moslem curses kismet. The Christian curses sin.

They all curse their accursedness; truly, all forms of accursedness are a deprivation of freedom.

They all curse their accursedness -- the only blessed curse. They all grumble against the ash, which has bound them to itself and is certain of its victory.

Truly, gamblers do not like one whose victory is assured in a game with people who are more inept.

---

[98] Cf. Gal. 3:26-29 and 4:21-31.

The Hindu does not curse the deprivation of freedom, but his vassalage to what is worse than himself. Nor does the Moslem curse the deprivation of freedom, but his vassalage to what is worse than himself. Nor does the Christian curse the deprivation of freedom, but his vassalage to what is worse than himself. None of them grumbles against their master as though he were their master, but as though he were a master inferior to themselves.

The world seeks masters. In tasting masters it falls beneath the heel of servants and, feeding on ashes, it tries to preserve its dignity only by grumbling.

I took counsel with myself and asked myself: "Can you cast karma behind you -- this towering mountain, as ancient as the world, and as weighty as the world -- can you cast it behind you?

"Can a drop of water really find its way into the light? Can the fire in the heart of the mountain bore its way through and break out on top, where the sun awaits it?"

Again I took counsel with myself and asked myself: "Can you develop a kismet for kismet? Can a cameleer save both himself and his camel from a sandstorm, and return on time from a route without oases?

"Can a son enter into his patrimony from a plenipotentiary father?

"Can the law-fulfiller become the law-giver?"

Again I took counsel with myself and asked myself: "Can you escape from this field of sins, where a single seed yields a hundred harvests?

"Can one, who has found a better field, really abandon the one that is worse?
"Can one, who has found out that his fellow wayfarer is a malefactor, really turn around and run away from him?"

But the fright within me retorts: "What if there is no other field? What if there is no other fellow-wayfarer?"

But the more courageous *I* within me replies: "When I speak of Brahma, am I not speaking of the other field? When I speak of Allah, am I not speaking of the other, fellow-wayfarer? When I speak of Christ, am I not speaking of salvation?"

O Heavenly Master, accept my soul as Your handmaiden. Lo, my only freedom is to serve one better than myself.

LXIX

"Unprofitable servants!"[99] Thus speaks the Lord of life and Vanquisher of death:

"Can you increase your stature by a single cubit?[100] Can you make a hair turn white or black?[101] And when you cannot do what is least, why do you worry about the rest?

---

[99] Cf. Matt. 25:30 and Luke 17:10.
[100] Cf. Matt. 6:27.
[101] Cf. Matt. 5:36.

"The master of a house, who hires servants, gives them a field and tools and food. Even so does the Heavenly Father provide for His servants!

"Unprofitable servants, God gives you the strength to serve; and it is not even you who serve, but God who serves through you.

"If you could perform a single good service without God, you would be gods, and God would not exist.

"If you could take a single life, and resurrect a single dead man, without God's presence, you would be gods and God would not exist.

"When you perform all your service, it is God who has performed the service, and it is you who are the unprofitable servants."

I said to my feet: "You do not walk by your own power;" and to my hands: "You do not create by your own power;" and to my nerves: "You do not sense by your own power;" and I said to my mind: "You do not reason by your own power."

Nor can all my caution lead me through a single night alive. Nor can all my toil add a single installment to my lifetime.

And to bread I said: "It is not you who nourish me, but the One who invisibly enters into me with you." And to light I said: "It is not you who illuminate me, but the One from whom even you have borrowed luminosity."

Sons of men, you are all unprofitable servants. Elements of nature, you are all unprofitable servants. Suns, stars and moons, you are all unprofitable servants.

All your service is in vain, unless someone stronger than you provides it.

All your promises are illusions, unless someone wealthier fulfills them.

All your cares are like thorns, that you sow in your way. They do not bring down rain, but make a drought more severe. They do not increase life, but amass weakness.

Unprofitable servants, convert your cares into prayers, just as ice is converted into flowing water, and you will reap an unexpected harvest. Pray to the Lord of the harvest, and then you will understand how vain and ruinous your cares were.

What does it profit for a shepherd's pipe to worry about how it will play? All its worries will not produce a single sound until a player places his mouth on it.

Look upon yourself as nothing; lay claim to nothing -- and everything will be given to you.[102]

And after you will have done so, you will sense that you are ceasing to be unprofitable servants and that you are becoming sons and heirs of a father. And the Father will clothe you in the gold and purple of His glory.

---

[102] Cf. Matt. 6:33.

LXX

Help me to be born anew, O consubstantial Trinity.

In vain do I try to clarify myself in the muddy river bed, wherein my life flows. I make a vow to You: I shall flow over dry stone, and shall no longer muddy myself. You will see Your face reflected in me, and will recognize it. Your angels will descend into me, and will not sense the descent.

Not a single willow will cast its shadow on my water, and not a single serpent will dare to enter my cool whirlpools.

Just help me to begin over again. I make a vow to You: I shall weave a new garment of new threads. I have tried long enough with my neighbors to sew new patches onto old garments. The patches fall off, the tatters fail apart, and our sordid nakedness makes us blush with shame.[103]

The wise *rishis* beneath the Himalayas speak of new births, which they say number more than the sands of the sea. But what good are all these births to me, which serve only as a gateway for me to leave one prison to enter another?

I beseech You for one birth only, for being born of the Spirit. I was born of water and baptized with water, and am creeping over the earth like muddy water.[104]

---

[103] Cf. Matt. 9:16.

[104] "Jesus answered, 'Most assuredly, I say to you, unless one is born of water and the Spirit, he cannot enter the kingdom of God.'" (John 3:5).

Indeed, being born of water is only a prophecy of being born of the Spirit, and baptism with water is only a prophecy of the baptism with fire.[105]

With water we are recruited as soldiers, but with the Spirit we are made victors.

Do not permit your soldier, my Lord, to fight for a lifetime and then completed his soldiering with defeat. Let the victor be born in me, who will not doubt even for a second that he is born for victory.

Water gives birth to an army inclined to defeat, while the Spirit gives birth to an army inclined to victory. Help me to be born anew. O consubstantial Trinity, so that there may appear in me the sort of man You had in Your mind before time. A man girded with Your strength, adorned with Your wisdom, illuminated with Your purity!

So that You might be entering my eyes, and not the world. So that my heart might yearn only for You.

And so that my soul might be impregnated by Your seed alone.

Do not abandon me, O Holy Trinity, to expire as an old man, to wear out as a threadbare garment, patched in vain and left unpatched.

The world has brought old age into my soul. It has stamped my entire soul and left its seals on her, so that from them she is suffering, agonizing, and -- dying.

---

[105] Cf. Luke 3:16 and 12:49-50.

Once my soul is born anew in my bones, my bones will also be rejuvenated. And there will be only one seal in my soul -- the seal of the gift of the Holy Spirit.[106] In vain will the world try to stamp its seal on me, to brand me as its own sheep -- it will find no place for its seal. For the one born anew will be filled with Your seal and Your life, O Life-creating Trinity.

LXXI

You have filled Yourself with peace, O Glory of the realms on high, and the anger of all lands cannot confound Your peace.

Among mortals peace is scarce, therefore anger has become arrogant.

In the bosom of arrogance anger makes its nest, and in the bosom of anger lies murder.[107]

All sins lead to murder, but none stands so close to murder as anger.

The one-eyed laws of the world do not punish anger, because they do not see that anger kills. But Your clairvoyant law, O Glory of the realms on high, calls anger murder.

I strove, in sunlight and moonlight, to penetrate the mystery of Your law. And once my striving began to

---

[106] "The seal of the gift of the Holy Spirit" are the words spoken by an Orthodox Priest as he uses holy chrism to anoint those baptized and to con-firm them in the faith.
[107] Cf. Matt. 5:21-26.

wear away all my worldly aspirations, I began to perceive how the anger of my neighbors was killing me.

The children of anger are slaves, while the children of peace are sons.

Therefore Your Wisdom vociferates and reiterates to people, telling them to be sons!

For a son looks into the face of his father, and directs his own face toward the face of his father. And when he sees peace in the father's face, how can he disfigure his own face with anger, without diverting his gaze away from his father?

Anger brings infirmity into both the one who is angry and the one against whom the anger is vented. And infirmity is the predecessor of death.

A wonderworker does not work miracles among the children of anger, for the children of anger bring infirmity into him.

My neighbors: why do you feel stronger among those who love you, and weaker among those whom your presence angers? Is it not because the former lengthen your life with love, and the latter shorten your life with anger?

Therefore I enjoy being constantly with You, O Glory of the realms on high. For only in Your presence am I neither murdering, nor being murdered by them.

Just as drop after drop of water erodes even the hardest stone, so does anger erode the life of two people.

Like a murderer waiting in ambush with a knife, so does anger lurk in a haughty heart.

Truly, arrogance knows that it is guilty; therefore it places anger at the gates, to act as its sentry.

Arrogance knows that it is sinful; therefore it has found itself an advocate in another sin.

Fill my heart with serenity, O Glory of the realms on high, with the serenity of the angels before Your throne. For serenity has no abode or resting place for anger.

Grant me the serenity of a son, and I shall be ashamed to become angry at slaves or to kill slaves. Armor me with Your peace, which the anger of the children of anger will not be able to confound.

LXXII

Deliver my soul from self-delusion, my God, so that my body may also be delivered from bodily sin.

Deliver my soul from foolish arrogance and burning anger, and my body will neither behave foolishly nor burn.

The soul designed the body to be a portrait of herself, to be the organ of her speech. The body is mute and inert, either for good or for evil, if the soul will not speak.

The body knows nothing of adultery, if the soul does not tell it. Adultery is carried out in the heart; the body only repeats in its clumsy way what has been woven with fine threads in the mysterious chambers of the heart.[108]

My neighbors, look upon a woman the way a woman looks upon herself and self-delusion will fall from your eyes like scales.[109] look upon every being from within that being, and you will look, not with desire, but with compassion. You, O God, have sanctified marriage, and You have also sanctified celibacy.[110]

Those, who have the wisdom and the strength to use all the life bestowed on them by You for serving You, You have blessed.

And those, who are unable to keep within themselves all the life given to them, You have blessed, so that they can share it and transfer it to new beings, through a wife.

Truly it is self-delusion for a man to think that a woman attracts him. Indeed, it is the unused life in a man -- which drives a man toward a woman, for life does not wish to remain unused. You are life, O my God, and life is light. You are light, O my God, and You do not wish to be hidden in darkness and kept from shining.

Blessed is the man, who knows You within himself, and gives free rein to You to shine in his soul and in his body.

It is not important, whether you shine in one body or in shared flesh -- You merely wish to shine and illuminate the world and to fill it with Your life and Your strength.

---

[108] Cf. Matt. 5:27-30.
[109] Cf. Acts 9:18.
[110] Cf. Matt. 19:3-12, John 2:1-11, and 1 Cor. 7.

Blessed is the woman from whose eyes self-delusion falls and who knows a man the way a man knows himself, the woman who rejects desire and fills herself with compassion. She too keeps life within herself, with fear and dignity, as though she were keeping heaven within herself.

Blessed is everyone who comes to know in due time that adultery defiles and kills life.

One does not fool around with God. It is safer to fool around with fire than with God.

Nor is life, which comes from God, a narcotic for instant stupefactions, after which self-delusion manifests itself again and again; while shame and humiliation fall like heavy stones on the heart, emptied of one demented desire.

Deliver my soul from self-delusion, my God, so that my body may also be delivered from bodily sin.

LXXIII

Guide my tongue, O Blessed Wisdom, so that it may not deviate from truth for the rest of my life. Remind me of Your presence, so that I may be afraid to utter falsehood. Encourage me with Your presence, so that I may freely speak the truth.

An oath bears witness to falsehood in the world. In the kingdom of truth oaths are unknown.[111]

---

[111] Cf. Matt. 5:33-37.

As out of a deep pit many wicked vapors escape, so out of self-deception all sins come forth, each with its own color and scent.

Out of self-deception comes arrogance; out of self-deception -- anger; out of self-deception -- bodily sin; out of self-deception -- deception. Deception has armed itself with oaths.

Falsehood curses with the truth, and thereby it acknowledges truth as essence, and itself as a shadow. Falsehood does not curse with falsehood, for nothingness does not lean on nothingness. In its feebleness falsehood looks for a support in truth. The more falsehood is disseminated, the more oaths are also disseminated.

Swearing an oath humiliates a truthful husband and kills a lying husband. Where oaths multiply, lies also multiply. A sinful mind always has a ready oath on its tongue. Lying eyes fend off with the tongue, but they cannot defend themselves. Whoever fabricates deception, also fabricates oaths.

The sons of adultery are the swiftest forgers of lies and oaths. For adultery itself is a lie and false oath in and of itself.

The daughters of adultery call upon God as witness, and God withdraws from the judgments of men, and with His absence He drives everything into falsehood.

Guide my heart, O Blessed Wisdom, and my tongue will also be guided.

Guide my mind, O Blessed Wisdom, and my tongue will also be guided.

Guide my soul with Your presence, and my tongue will forget all oath-swearing.

What is the value of justifying myself before men, my God, if I stand accused before You?

I shall slow down my tongue and shall cease to swear oaths, even though I remain guilty before men.

Rightness before You fills the heart with gladness. Rightness before men fills the heart with sadness. O my God, I am Your living oath, that You will be with me to the end. It is better for me to be at peace with You than with the world. Truly, war with the world is easier than war with You.

O my God, my God, I am your living oath that You will be with me to the end.[112]

LXXIV

The Father looks from Heaven and sees me covered with wounds from the injustice of men, and says: "Do not take revenge."[113]

On whom shall I take revenge, O Lord? On a portion of the flock on its way to slaughter?

---

[112] Cf. Matt. 28:20.
[113] Cf. Matt. *5:38-42* and Rom. 12:19.

Does a physician take revenge on patients, for cursing him from their death bed?

On whom shall I take revenge? On the snow, for melting, or on the grass, for withering? Does a gravedigger take revenge on those descending into the grave?

On whom shall I take revenge? On simpletons, for thinking that they can do evil to someone else in the world besides themselves? Does a teacher take revenge on illiterate children for not knowing how to read?

Eternity bears me witness, that all those who are quick to avenge are slow to read and comprehend the mysteries of vengeance.

Time bears me witness, that all those who have taken revenge, have accumulated poison in themselves, and with poison they have blotted themselves out of the book of the living.

In what way can you avengers boast before your adversaries, except by being able to repeat their evil? Are you not thereby saying: "We are no better than you?"

God bears me witness: both you and your adversaries are equally reckless and equally incapable of good.

I have seen a cherry tree stripped of its bark and set fire to by children, yet it gave its ripe fruit to those same children.

And I have seen cows, which men tormented with heavy burdens, patiently give milk to those same men.

And tears welled up in my eyes: why is nature more compassionate to men than man is to his fellow man?

Nature bears me witness, avengers: a man is more powerful than those who do him evil only when he is powerless to repeat their evil deeds.

There is no end to vengeance, and the heirs continue the work of their fathers and then depart, leaving it unfinished.

Evil races along the wide road, and from each new duel it gains strength and territory, and it multiplies its retinue.

A wise man gets off the road, and leaves evil to race [with itself].

A piece of bread silences a barking dog more swiftly than a pile of stones does.

He who taught men: an eye for an eye -- also taught them how they would all be left blind.

On whom shall I take revenge, my heavenly Father? On a portion of the flock on its way to slaughter?
Ah, how wretched are all evildoers and avengers! Truly, they resemble a flock on its way to be slaughtered and, unaware of where they are heading, they butt horns with each other and perpetrate a slaughter before the slaughter.

I do not seek vengeance, my Father; I do not seek vengeance, but seek rather that You grant me a sea of tears, so that I can bewail the wretchedness of those who are on their way to slaughter, unaware of where they are heading.

LXXV

Bless my enemies, O Lord. Even I bless them and do not curse them.[114]

Enemies have driven me into Your embrace more than friends have. Friends have bound me to earth, enemies have loosed me from earth and have demolished all my aspirations in the world.

Enemies have made me a stranger in worldly realms and an extraneous inhabitant of the world. Just as a hunted animal finds safer shelter than an unhunted animal, so have I, persecuted by enemies, found the safest sanctuary, having ensconced myself beneath Your tabernacle, where neither friends nor enemies can slay my soul. Bless my enemies, O Lord. Even I bless them and do not curse them.

They, rather than I, have confessed my sins before the world.

They have flagellated me, whenever I have hesitated to flagellate myself.

They have tormented me, whenever I have tried to flee torments.

---

[114] Cf. Matt. 5:43-48.

They have scolded me, whenever I have flattered myself. They have spat upon me, whenever I have filled myself with arrogance.

Bless my enemies, O Lord. Even I bless them and do not curse them.

Whenever I have made myself wise, they have called me foolish.

Whenever I have made myself mighty, they have mocked me as though I were a dwarf.

Whenever I have wanted to lead people, they have shoved me into the background.

Whenever I have rushed to enrich myself, they have prevented me with an iron hand.

Whenever I thought that I would sleep peacefully, they have wakened me from sleep.

Whenever I have tried to build a home for a long and tranquil life, they have demolished it and driven me out.

Truly, enemies have cut me loose from the world and have stretched out my hands to the hem of Your garment.

Bless my enemies, O Lord. Even I bless them and do not curse them.

Bless them and multiply them; multiply them and make them even more bitterly against me -- so that my fleeing to You may have no return; so that all hope in men may be scattered like cobwebs; so that absolute serenity may begin to reign in my soul;

so that my heart may become the grave of my two evils twins: arrogance and anger;

so that I might amass all my treasure in heaven;[115]

ah, so that I may for once be freed from self-deception, which has entangled me in the dreadful web of illusory life.

Enemies have taught me to know -- what hardly anyone knows -- that a person has no enemies in the world except himself.

One hates his enemies only when he fails to realize that they are not enemies, but cruel friends.

It is truly difficult for me to say who has done me more good and who has done me more evil in the world: friends or enemies.

Therefore bless, O Lord, both my friends and my enemies.

A slave curses enemies, for he does not understand. But a son blesses them, for he understands.

For a son knows that his enemies cannot touch his life. Therefore he freely steps among them and prays to God for them.

Bless my enemies, O Lord. Even I bless them and do not curse them.

---

[115] Matt. 6:19-21.

LXXVI

At dawn when I awake, my seemly thoughts fly straight to You; the first stirrings of my soul reach for Your smile; the first whisper in my ear -- is Your name, the first surprise I encounter -- is You, beside me.

Like a young boy after a nightmare, who embraces his mother and rejoices because the dream did not separate him from his mother, so also do I, when waking, embrace You and rejoice because my journey in sleep has not distanced me from Your hand.

How unkind I am toward You, my love! Shame devours me because I have been so unkind toward You. Whereas You do not separate Yourself from me for a single second, I divorce myself from You in sleep for hours at a time. Therefore I curse sleep and my sleeping, and I marvel at the heavenly hosts, who never take their eyes off You either day or night.

Sleep makes me weary, but You give me rest. There is no rest for one who is weary unless he looks at You, nor is there any sweetness for one embittered unless he converses with You, nor is there any health for one who is sick unless he touches Your hand, nor is there any purification for one who is impure unless he bathes in Your light.

I hasten through deserted streets to Your church, I hasten and greet no one in the empty streets. Everyone is sleeping and in their dreams they torment themselves far away from You, yet You sit at every bedside and await the return of souls from the distance.

Shame devours me, my love, when I consider how unkind the souls of men are toward You, and how profoundly they separate themselves from their Life.

Even the animals in the mountain forests awake at dawn, and You stand beside them and shepherd them. The forest creatures are thinking about food, they think about food early in the morning even as I do. Indeed, I too think at dawn about my food, and I know that my hunger can only be satisfied with You.

Through the deserted streets I hasten, my Glory, to seek Your glory. I hear both the *muezzin* calling from the minaret and the church bell summoning the faithful to church. And in my thoughts I raise myself and survey every place on earth to see how many sons of men have left their senseless wandering in sleep and met with the One Who Is, who is far distant from senseless sleep.

The holy ascetics in their monastery cells and hermitage caves have risen, and have already been conversing with You for a long time. These holy monastics have risen, whose soul never even lies down, but like a candle burns upright before You day and night.

Bless, O Lord, all these prayerful ascetics, who cense the slumbering world with their life like incense.

Thousands upon thousands of souls bid farewell to their bodies at dawn. And when the sun is born, it will burn like a funerary candle over the thousands of deceased.

And I watch You, my love, keeping vigil beside the thousands dying as you wait for them to call upon Your name. And behold, some of them repent for the whole slumber of their life and cry out to You for help.

Bless, O Lord, all penitents at death, and respond to their cry.

Through deserted streets I hasten, my Glory, and I enter into church to hymn and extol Your glory. And I stand alone in the church, packed with You and Your angels. And I fall down on my knees and pray to You with tears:

Awaken all the slumbering souls to Yourself, O celestially-supported Lord, all the slumbering souls of my brethren and my people!

The souls of sinners have become heavy and flabby, and have descended near to Hades. O eternally vigilant love, awaken them before death shoves them yet another step deeper into sleep, into everlasting sleep -- into the dreadful sleep which ends with You not keeping vigil.

LXXVII

At noon the children gather at the lake, to bathe in the sun and the water.

O Lord, how the whole of nature marvels at innocence! Strained and pained laborers in the presence of sinners -- the lake and the sun are transfigured in the presence of children. What a magnificent temple of the Lord the lake becomes, when children are in it, and what an inspired high priest the sun becomes, when its rays cross the rays of children's souls.

"Let the children come to me," whispers the whole of nature, "and you will understand that I myself am also a child. To the soulless I seem to be soulless, to saints I am an altar. Whoever seeks the beast in me, will be sent a beast; whoever seeks God in me, will be shown God. Sinners call me a slaughterhouse, the righteous call me a sacrificial altar. Only to innocence do I manifest myself as innocence, and only to children of God do I reveal myself as a child of God."

"Let the children come to Me," exclaims the Son of the Virgin, and only children come to Him.[116] Those who prevent children from coming to the Son of God, will be liable to the fires of hell. For neither do they themselves come to Him nor do they allow others to come to Him.[117]

"Why children, O Lord, why do You seek children?" those who are made and not born ask the One who was begotten and not made. Such people are made and not born, like statues of stone, and they are moved by the winds of the world. But the One who is begotten and not made moves with life within, and the winds of the world flee from Him.

"Because I Myself am also a child, for this reason I seek children. Impostors see an impostor in Me, atheists see an atheist, and those in authority see in Me one who usurps authority. The Pharisees ask 'Who is this man?' and they cannot resolve the question, while the wise of this world pursue Me into their own worldly wisdom.

"Only children recognize Me, for I too am a child. As a child I am not My own, and as a child I do not seek glory for Myself. As a child I do not think anything on My own, I do not speak anything on My own, and I do not

---

[116] Cf. Mark 10:13-16.
[117] Cf. Matt. 23:13.

do anything on My own. Instead, like a child, I think what My Father taught
Me, and I speak what I hear, and I do what I see.[118]

"Children cease to be children, but I never cease being a child. Children cease to be children because of their wicked guides, who prevent them from continuing to sojourn with Me and teach them the time-worn wisdom of the world. But I do not cease to be a child, because I nourish Myself with the eternally youthful wisdom of heaven.

"Blessed are those who in old age rid themselves of their wicked guides and the wisdom of those guides, which makes one old, sick, and dead. Whoever turns to Me, even if he has been made old by the world, I shall make him a child and as an eternal child he will reign in My kingdom, to which the elders of the world have no access.

"I tell you that My kingdom is a kingdom of children.

"Truly, those who are made will not see the light of the Kingdom of God, but only those who are begotten. Whatever is Mine, whatever is as I am, this will be with Me.

"The statues of stone, which the winds of the world move, will be smashed, and their dust will be the sport of winds. But the children, who move with life within, will enter into eternal life."

O Resplendent Lord, Eternal Child of the Holy Triad, help me with Your innocence, the greatest strength in all realms, to be born of the Holy Spirit.

---

[118] Cf. John 5:19-23,30,43.

May I not be like a stone statue, made by this world, to be smashed and scattered into the wind.

May I rather be like a born youth, inseparable from You in eternity, O Prince of Innocence and of all innocents.

LXXVIII

In the evening the stardust begins to sparkle above my head, and I sense the abyss over which my life is dangling. And with a trembling soul I stretch out my hands to You and cry out: O Lord, the terrifying world has enveloped me from every direction, as the sandy desert envelops a small tiny oasis.

I shall not be able to hold out, if You do not brace me with Your strength. The sand will cover over my green pasture, it will clog the spring in the pasture, and the sand dunes will rise above the palm trees. And beneath the sands a heart that has loved you will be reduced to dust, and the dust will stick to the hoofs of camels. And the sand will stop the mouth that has known only a single song, a hymn to You the Almighty. And out of the millions of years of life one day of life will be erased, as though it had never existed. And the weighty wheels of the universe will clatter on, no longer even caring that it has turned a day of life into a grain of sand.

But You are stronger than the world, O Lord my God, and You will lend Your servant a cherubic sword of flame, with which I shall repel the onslaught of the world on my life.

I shall not be saved, even if I am as equally strong as the world, much less so if I am less strong than the world. One who is equal to the world does not overcome the world, nor does the world fear him; instead the world of trivialities teaches one less strong than itself to prepare a grave for himself. Yet I shall be saved if I am more powerful than the world, and conquer the world.

My self-delusion portrays the world to me as an awesome power. When self-delusion dies within me and truth begins to dawn, I see and I know that a single drop of Your living fire is more powerful than a universe of ashes. Not even the entire universe has the strength to nourish a single blade of grass, if it does not receive that strength from You.

He who was born of Truth and sent by Truth easily conquers the world.[119] The world flees before Him as a shadow flees before the sun.

Fear of the world is the nourishment, day and night, of those who have separated themselves from Truth. Made by the world, they have become the world's puppets, with which the world plays, as a child plays with his toys. The children of Truth are begotten of Truth and do not fear those made dead.
Help me, my God, to conquer the world within myself; and I shall easily conquer the world outside me.

I shall not become arrogant by conquering the world, for the victory is Yours and not mine.

I shall let You increase, while I shall decrease, and like a child I shall cling to Your garment.

---

[119] Cf. John 16:33.

I shall let Your Word take up His abode in my body, and I shall expel from myself all the powerless words, taught to me by the world. Your Word is innocence, and wisdom, and power. He will annihilate what is made in me, and will help me be born.

The body, which the Word of God inhabits, is no longer a body made by the world, but a body conceived and commenced by the Holy Spirit. Enslaved by the world, my soul has woven me a slave's body as well. Therefore both my soul and my body tremble in terror of the world.

Illumine my soul, my Luminous God, and she will take courage and free herself of the world. She will become a sonlike soul, who will know how to weave a sonlike body, to be a temple of the Son of God.[120]

When the stardust begins to sparkle above my head, I call upon You for help, my Most Holy God, and I do not fear all the worlds, just as a son does not fear the servants in his father's house.

LXXIX

People have become bad, and so they say: "What does the Lord do for us?"
The Lord gives life to every body; the Lord gives a face to every creature. The Lord is as tenderhearted as a child, and selfishness and gloominess are unknown to Him.

---

[120] Cf. Cor. 16-17, 2 Cor. 6:16, and John 2:21.

The Lord gives to everyone whatever one asks of Him.[121] The Lord fills His eternity with giving, and yet you say: "What does the Lord give to us?" You would not even have been able to pose this question, if the Lord had not given you the power to do so.

The Lord collects the tears of those who mourn in the palms of His hands. The Lord visits captives. The Lord sits at the bedside of the sick.

The Lord keeps vigil over perilous paths, and keeps watch over the depths of the sea, and yet you say: "What does the Lord do for us?"

Whatever you ask of the Lord, He also gives you. But because you began to seek more from the world than from the Lord, you feel deluded in your hopes, and so you say: "What does the Lord do for us?"

Like a good host, the Lord sets His table and awaits His guests. The Lord listens attentively for knocking, and is quick to open the door to every guest.[122] Around His table are clustered undreamed-of mansions; at His table are many seats. Whoever strikes His door and knocks, will not be turned away, and yet you say: "Why did the Lord not open when we knocked?" Because you knocked at the door of the Lord with doubt, but at the door of the world with faith.[123]

The Lord stands at the door of your soul with a broom, ready, at your invitation, to clean the horrendous filth out of your soul, to make your newly-cleaned soul fragrant with incense and fragrance, and to adorn her

---

[121] Cf. Matt. 7:7-12.
[122] Cf. Luke 11:9-13.
[123] Cf. James 1:5-8, Matt. 21:20-22 and Mark 11:23-24.

with virginal jewelry --the Lord is standing and waiting for your invitation.[124]

At the edge of your heart the Lord is standing with a tall candle that burns without smoking or melting. The Lord is standing and waiting at your invitation, to bring the candle into your heart and enlighten it, to burn up all the fear in your heart, all its selfish passions and all its ugly desires, and to drive out of your heart all the smoke and foul stench.

At the edge of your mind the Lord is standing with His wisdom and with His tongue, ready, at your invitation, to enter into it and drive out all its foolish thoughts, all its filthy fancies, and all its mistaken notions, and to erase from your mind all nonexistent images -- the Lord is standing and waiting to introduce His reason, His seals, and His words.

Yet you say: "Where is the Lord?" At the edge of your life. Therefore your life has become hunchbacked. If the Lord were in the center, where He was in the beginning and where His rightful place is, your life would be upright and you would see the Lord, and you would not be asking: "Where is the Lord?"

You have become bad, therefore you ask: "Where is the Lord?"

The Lord is too good, therefore the bad do not recognize Him.

The Lord is too translucent, therefore the dusty do not see Him.

The Lord is too holy, therefore the unholy do not perceive Him.

---

[124] Cf. Rev. 3:20.

If there are not enough people, who will confess the name of the Lord, the Lord will manifest Himself through objects.

If even the stars of heaven forget the name of the Lord, it will not be forgotten by the countless hosts of angels in heaven.

The weaker the confession of the Lord's name in one realm, the stronger it is in another. Neither can the uttering of the name of God be decreased, nor can it be increased. If one brook dries up, another will begin to rise, and thus -- the sea maintains the same level.

LXXX

The cypress is green in both summer and winter. Basil is fragrant *in* both summer and winter. Lambs are slain in both summer and winter.

Beware of wolves, when they attack you, one from the front and another from behind. But be even more wary of two sins: fearing sinners and scorning sinners. For your greenness will vanish like the greenness of a willow. And your fragrance will turn into a stench. And your humility will become arrogance. And sinners will call you their namesakes.

You who are righteous: sin is weakness, and to be afraid of sinners is to be afraid of weaklings. A sinner is terrified of the dead righteous man within himself, and twice as terrified of a living righteous man outside himself.

Do not be terrified of someone, who is twice as terrified of you.

Is not the Lord the courage of the righteous? Is not the Lord Almighty the general of the righteous hosts? Truly minute is the righteousness of those who stand with the Al-mighty and yet fear the all-unmighty.

If your justice is God's justice, your power is a divine power. In the beginning divine power seems to sinners to be weakness, for it is excessively meek, gentle and longsuffering. But in the end, when divine victory comes, sinners see with horror, that their house has been undermined by underground water, and is sinking down with no way back.

Like grass, God's victory grows slowly and silently. But once it has grown, one can no longer trample it or mow it.

Sinners are a flock without a shepherd; you are not. And if your shepherd leaves you, he does not leave you to abandon you, but to sift you in a fine sifter. Your shepherd will return soon, and you will die of shame for betraying him.

You who are righteous, sin is a sickness, and to despise sinners is to scorn the sick. He who gives of His own health to the sick, multiplies his own health.

Scorning sinners undermines the health of one who is healthy.

Sin sits at the table of those who are afraid to sit at the table of a sinner. Sin enters the home of those who are afraid to enter the home of a sinner.

Whoever turns back from his way, in order to avoid meeting a sinner, returns home laden with sin.

At every gate of your soul post a sentry, lest arrogance invade your temple. For if it enters, it will at once blow out the candles of all your virtues; and you will be like a wineskin filled with wine, when it is punctured with a needle.

Brief is *this* day of life, but true life knows no night.

Whoever dies of sin during this day, will die a death that knows no day.

You who are righteous, pass one course after the next without a break. Whoever completes one course in righteousness, will be enrolled by the Lord in more advanced and more difficult ones. The sinner suffers from a lack of education, the righteous man suffers from studying. But truly the travail of the righteous man is sweeter than the travail of the sinner, just as returning to one's homeland is sweeter than residing in a foreign country.

O compassionate Heavenly Mother of God, protect all those who have set out on the way of righteousness, lest they fear sinners and lest they scorn sinners.

Lest their fear make them God-betrayers, and lest their scorning of sinners make them manslayers.

Lest their quasi-righteousness be merely a pinnacle, from which they will fall even further downward to their destruction.

LXXXI

I was a shepherd for sheep, and You elevated me to be a shepherd for men.

I used to find green pasture for the sheep, and they were satisfied. I offer You as nourishment to men, and many do not even try you.

My heart is convulsed within me from sorrow, my Lord, and my eyes are constantly moistened with tears, because many do not try You, but instead they seek their nourishment in the fields of famine.

Not in that direction, my brethren, not in that direction. Those are the fields of famine where you are heading; your hunger will grow greater. And in demon-crazed hunger you will hunt each other and will devour one another, and your hunger will not be satisfied.

Sheep are nourished with what is from God, but you are men, intended to be nourished with God. If men were also to be nourished with the nourishment of sheep, why would God have created both men and sheep?

What are sheep except grass -- the nourishment with which they are nourished. But you are invited to be gods, therefore God offers Himself to you as nourishment.[125]

---

[125] Cf. John 6:27-58.

O my Lord, I kneel down before You and entreat Your mercy. Faith among Your priests has grown cold, therefore many people do not try You. Your rich pasture lies there scarcely touched by grazing. A good shepherd for sheep is not a good shepherd for men. Why did you not leave me, to be good at something small, rather than designate me to be bad at something great?

Even when I was a shepherd of sheep, I was Your priest. With my shepherd's staff I would overturn every stone and blade of grass, and I would lie on my stomach on the ground and listen to the breathing of the earth, and I would lie on my back and watch the awesome fires of heaven. I would touch the dewy leaves in the mountain forest with my forehead, and would hug the tall fir trees that had been struck by lightning with compassion. And I used to read your name etched with fire all over the earth, and I used to feel every footstep beneath me burning and saying: "I am the altar of the Most High." And I used to fill all the valleys, all the groves, and all the pathways with my amazement at Your majesty. But once I grew up I discovered, with unutterable shuddering, that You are even closer to me than I used to suspect in the fields of my childhood. I discovered, O Lord, that even I myself am the earth, in which you burn and speak. I discovered, my Master, that I am the stranger within myself, and You are the Lord and master of the house.

And this discovery filled me with a horror, which pierced me to the marrow of my bones with an icy chill. I said to myself: "Have you not therefore sullied someone else's home and not your own? And have you not brought shame upon another rather than on yourself? Instead of insulting yourself, have you not insulted the master of the house, in whose home you are a guest? And instead of slinging mud on your own place, have you not slung mud on some sort of sun within you?"

What sort of baptism can wash away my disgrace from You? What sort of repentance can rectify my sin against You? Help me to annihilate myself, so that there is no "me," and so that I may be born anew, as a youth without a past. Help me, my heavenly Father.

The pagan idols expect a certain measure of wisdom from their priests. How much more wisdom is necessary for a priest of the Living God!

The idols expect a certain measure of purity. How much more radiant purity is expected of one who serves the God of gods!

The idols expect a certain measure of strength from their servers. With how much more strength must one gird himself, who is a server of the All-Powerful Almighty?

O my Most High heavenly Father, purity my life and make it a sacrifice on Your sacrificial altar. When I was a shepherd of lambs, I used to cry when they wanted to sacrifice a single lamb. Make me as innocent as a lamb, and consume me in flames on Your altar. I promise You that I shall not cry, O my Lord and my God.

LXXXII

The unbelievers have girded for war against the Lord of heaven and earth -- like dry leaves against the mountain wind! As long as the wind is soundless, one hears the rustling of the leaves. But once the wind begins to howl, it will scatter the leaves over the marshes and roadways, and left there, leaf upon leaf, they will perish like rumors and will be blinded with mud.

For an unbeliever feels strong in a crowd and makes noise. In solitude fear and weakness devour him. But when a believer is in a crowd, he shares the weakness of the crowd, while in solitude he shares power with You; therefore solitude is his strength and his song.

Against whom do you wage war, you lunatics? Is it against the One who kindles suns with His thought, and goads His flocks of suns and stars with His staff? Truly, it would be a less ridiculous war for the willows to declare war on the thunder, or for the bach fish to carry out a war against the awesome condors.

You have forged weapons, with which you crush one another, and so you have risen up to battle against Him with the same weaponry. But behold, He can walk over your swords like soft moss. Nor is he intimidated by your fortresses any more than He is by your graves.

You have concocted petty words, with which you insult and humiliate one another, and so you think that with your petty words you will humiliate the One who alone knows what a word is and whence it comes? Indeed, He created your vocal cords in your throat, and expanded your lungs beneath those cords, and cut open your mouth and attached your tongue in your mouth. Truly, it would be less ridiculous for a shepherd's flute in a shop to rebel against its master craftsman, or for the strings on a harp to rebel against the hand that plucks them.

You have declared war not against God but against yourselves, and God watches your suicide with compassion. Dry leaves are declaring war on wheels of iron!

The more seriously you war against Him, the more unimpededly is He drawn out of you. The Lord withdraws His strength out of you, as well as His beauty, His health, His wisdom and His blessedness. This is the way the Most High Lord wars with His adversaries.

What remains of you, embattled battlers, once the Lord has drawn out from you what is His? Does anything remain other than weakness, ugliness, sickness, madness and wretchedness? The Lord will not take from you anything of what is yours. And what is yours is weakness. And once He takes away His power, which you are abusing, He will leave you with your own sepulchral weakness, which can be neither used nor abused.

The Lord will pull His health out of you, and your blood will be transformed into sweat, and your odor will be pleasing to worms, an odor that will cause cities to close their gates.

The Lord will return His wisdom to Himself, and in your madness you will run through the groves, and quarrel with caves.

The Lord will retract His blessedness and His peace to Himself, and even the springs will be frightened by your anxiety and will flee; and the vines in the hills will wither from your wretchedness, and the earth in the fields will return its fertility back to the earth.

This is the way the Most High Lord wars with His adversaries.

Like a child, He is powerless to do evil. He does not return evil for evil, for He is destitute when it comes to evil. Instead He merely gathers His good gifts and walks off with them, away from the one who gnashes his teeth at Him. And the Lord leaves the unbelievers to be by themselves. And they disintegrate like worm-eaten wood, from which the moisture has evaporated and throughout which worms wend their way for food, as through a deserted home.

Thus does it also happen with a people, that declares war on the Life-Giver.

I have told my people -- remember: such is the victory of the Life-Giver, and such is the defeat of the godless.

LXXXIII

People carry on foolish conversations as soon as they move away from Your presence, my Wisdom. Those without faith speak about works, and those without works speak about faith.[126]

---

[126] A fierce debate arose in Western Christendom at the time of the Protestant Reformation in the sixteenth century regarding faith vs. works and their relative role in the justification and salvation of

Each disparages what he does not have, and what he does have he proclaims throughout the marketplace.

While You, O Lord, are filling my home with Your life-creating breath, I always forget to ask which is more important -- faith or works? As soon as I offend You and feel abandoned by You, I angrily enter into people's discussions, and support one side or the other.

For without You I am like a weather vane on a chimney that rattles in the direction of the wind. When the wind of faith rises in my soul, I stand with those who have abandoned works and championed faith; when the wind of activity rises in my soul, I support the side of those who have abandoned faith and championed works.

But in Your all-calming presence there is no wind, no swaying, no "doing things." I neither feel faith nor see works; instead I feel and see only You, the living God. In truth, You are not my faith but my vision. And You are not my doing, but I am Your doing. And again I say: You are not my faith but I am Your faith, and Your trust.

---

man. Martin Luther held that justification (the act whereby God, in virtue of the Sacrifice of Christ, acquits a man of punishment due to his sins and in His mercy treats him as though he were righteous) was granted to men in response to the disposition of faith alone and that it brought with it the imputation to the sinner of the merits of Christ. This was in contradistinction to the emphasis by the Roman catholic Church on the role of one's own good works and personal sanctification in his justification and salvation by God. Bishop Nikolai, like the Orthodox Church in general, regards this debate between Catholicism and Protestantism as nugatory hair-splitting although he would agree with the apostle James that "faith by itself, if it does not have works, is dead" (James 2:18) and that faith is evidenced by works, and works by faith (cf. James 2:14-26).

And so I teach those around me who are carrying on the debate: whoever has true faith in the Living God prefers to remain silent. And whoever performs a true work of God, prefers to remain silent. But whoever shuts up his faith with his mind, gladly squabbles about faith. And whoever does his own work and not God's gladly boasts of his works.

Deep is the tranquility of the soul in a man of faith, deeper than the tranquility at the bottom of the sea. For God's Wisdom is born and resides in deep tranquility.

Deep is the tranquility in the tongue of one who does God's work, deeper than the tranquility of the iron in the heart of a mountain. For whoever does the work of another listens to instructions and carries them out, moreover he listens, and has no time to speak.

I speak believing in works: Is not my prayer a working and reworking of my very self? Is not the whole world within me, from beginning to end, together with all the world's poverty and impurity? Truly I am not without works, when I sweat and weep in prayer, but am immersed in the weighty task of helping the poor in my soul -- healing the sick and casting out the unclean spirits from my soul.

I speak believing in faith: Do I not awaken faith in my neighbors through the good works that I do?

Is not my work in the world the song of my faith, the psalm of one saved among the unsaved? Who would stop the song in the throat of a brimming soul? Who would stop a brimming spring from flowing? Would the nymphs who guard the spring quarrel with the nymphs in the spring's stream over which water is more beneficial? Truly, if there were no spring, there would be no stream.

O my Lord, do not go far away from me, lest my soul succumb to meaningless quarrels. Silence in Your presence expands my soul; discussions in Your absence shrink her and expend her to the thinness of a boon of flax.

I listened last time to the people squabbling, and You waved your hands and went far away. Indeed, those who truly have faith do not squabble with those who are true doers of Your work. This is the quarrel of servants with little faith and much ill will. Those who are of little faith squabble with the errand boys of the world. They are a dried-up spring quarrelling with a dried-out stream.

While they were full, they both used to sing a true song of joy, and joyfully used to hail each other.

But this is a malicious believer quarrelling with a malicious doer. What do I have in common with them? What ties me to them except compassion, which flows forth from Your radiance?

Fill the house of my soul, O Life-Creating Spirit, so that I may become blind and not see angry squabbling people, and so that I may be deaf to their foolish discussion.

They have slipped away from You, my Joy, therefore they engage in foolish discussions.

I bow down and beseech You, tie my soul across the thousands of sunbeams to You, lest she slip away from You, and plunge into the cold abyss.

LXXXIV

Those who educate by blinding rather than by enlightening --what will You do with them, O Lord?

They turn Your children away from You, and prevent them from approaching Your Grace, for they say: "'The Lord' is an archaic term of your dead grandparents. It is an old amulet, which your grandparents used to wear but they have died off. We shall teach you how to till the earth, how to fatten the body, and how to dig for gold, which shines more brilliantly than the dead Lord." What will You do with these corrupters of Your children, O Lord?

"I shall do nothing to them, for they have done everything to curse their own seed and breed. Truly, they have prepared a worse judgment for themselves and their people than the scribes and Sadducees. For they had the example of these latter, and failed to learn from it.

"In their old age, they will hear sabers rattling at their threshold, and will be dying of hunger, bald and gaunt, and they will not dare to poke their heads out of their door to warn their students. How will they warn them, when My name has been expelled from their brigand hearts? What will they even say to warn them, since they prepared their students for this in their own abysmal stupidity, which accompanies everyone whom I do not accompany?" What will happen to them, O Lord?

"It will be worse for them than for the Babylonians, when in their might they used to worship blood and gold, and used to teach their children to worship them also.

"First will come hunger, such as even Babylon never knew. And then war, for the sake of plundering bread, from which they will return defeated. And then an internecine slaughter and burning of cities and towns. And then diseases, which the hands of physicians will not dare to touch. And the teachers will be flogged with whips and goaded to be the gravediggers of their students, whose stenchful corpses fill all the roadways."

Those who lead the people are not leading the people, but are misleading the people -- what will You do with them, O my Lord? "They are leading the people astray for the sake of their own profit, and once the people arise and rise up, these leaders will step down from power and consume their ill-gotten gains in peace. They accuse their adversaries, and yet follow in their steps. Their clamor prevents a wise man from getting a word in edgeways.

"They flatter idiots and bullies just to attain the first places. They write books daily and expose the wickedness of their kinsmen, in order to conceal their own wickedness.

"They do not teach the people the truth, but feed them lies the year round.

"They are incapable of doing the people justice, so instead they intimidate them by scaring them with a worse injustice of times past.

"They pillage for themselves and their friends, for they know that they are not long for this world."

What will You do with them, O righteous Lord?

"They have done everything themselves, and I have nothing to do, except to leave them to themselves. Truly, they will not consume their gains in peace, but will spend it on the funeral feasts of their relatives.

"They will be impoverished, and mice will scurry through their torn shirts. They will dream of rebellions by those who have been deluded and looted, and they will arise at midnight, terrified and soaked with sweat. Their life will be long, so that their punishment may be longer.

"They will live to see their house in flames, and will flee their own land, hungry and sickly, and will not dare to utter their own names in the presence of anyone.

"They will see foreigners in their land, and will beg them for a piece of bread.

"It will be worse for their country than it was for the Roman Empire. For they had Rome for an example, and did not learn from it.

"It will be worse for their nation which was born of them, than it was for the Jewish nation. For they had the example of the Jewish nation, and did not learn from it.

"They will hear their names being cursed, and will not dare to poke their heads out the window.

"They will see their people, being led away bound in columns, and will be afraid for themselves.

"And they will hear, both when asleep and when awake, their name being cursed, and they will shiver -- they will shiver but will be unable to die."

O Great and Fearful Lord, all Your ways are grace and truth. What will You do with those who were blinded, misled, deceived and despoiled?

"I wait, to see who will cry out to Me -- and I will respond.

"As long as there is crying out on earth, there will also be an echo in heaven.

"I am the One who is closest to everyone on earth. I give Myself to everyone who desires Me; I withdraw Myself from everyone who does not acknowledge Me. Without Me the world is a pile of ashes. And without Me people are feebler than ashes."

LXXXV

Wherever a king is found, there is also a kingdom. A king without a kingdom is not a king, nor is a widowed kingdom a kingdom.

"The kingdom of heaven is within you,"[127] said the Royal Son, and joy has illuminated all those wayfarers

---

[127] Cf. Luke 17:21.

in the cemeteries, who have understood this heavenly message.

A Moslem does not believe that You ever touch the filthy earth. The pagan sees You entirely composed of earth. The Royal Son knows the royal way, and manifests You in purest earth. In purest earth He even clothed Himself and came down to bring luminescence and essence.[128]

O my King, You are nearer to me than my breath and dwell deeper within me than my thoughts.

What is my breath except something that enters into me from outside and leaves? Even before my lungs began breathing You were inside me. You knew of me while I was still in my father's loins. Even before the creation of the world You thought about me.[129]

What are my thoughts except the impressions of external objects, impressions which enter my mind like threads in a loom, where they are woven and brought together, disjoined and lost? All objects are outside my mind, and objects do not enter my mind but only their impressions.

However You are the only reality of my mind, with which my mind is also born. And You were in me before

---

[128] "And the Word became flesh and dwelt among us, and we beheld His glory, the glory as of the only begotten of the Father, hill of grace and truth" (John 1:14). "In Him was life, and the life was the light of men" (John 1:4).

[129] "He was in the beginning with God. An things were made through Him, and without Hirn nothing was made that was made" (John 1:2-3).

any impression was; You were in contact with me before I had contact with any object.

From the time I first heard the glad tidings of the King, I have spread out my soul like a canopy over most precious treasures and have sought You and Your Kingdom within her. I have spread her out and I see no end or bottom to her. I can neither reach all her height, nor descend into all her vaults.

I have discovered radiant rays, which indicate some sun in the distance. I have discovered the golden columns of a temple, but nowhere do I see any end to the temple.

I smell the fragrant scent of a censer's incense, but I cannot glimpse a royal throne.

The more I keep trying and discover, the more I see the One who is hidden.
You placed unimagined mysteries in me, O Lord of countless hosts. In each of Your soldiers Your royal radiance shines.

Just as a sun does not exist without radiant rays, so is the King not without His angels, His radiant rays.

You bring infinity with Yourself, my King, and You bring infinity into my soul.
You cloak Yourself with eternity as with a mantle, my King, and with this mantle you cloak my soul.

The Spirit creates His own Where and When, and is not dependent on His creations.

O Lord, Most Rich, I am discovering myself apart from the senses when I gaze into my soul. What immense wealth You have accumulated into this paltry earthen vessel!

Truly, I am to blame, if I feel poor. I am to blame, if I feel mortal.
It is my own suicide, if I feel that I am a slave of the world and of worldly self-deception.

Wherever You are, there also is the kingdom of heaven; and wherever the kingdom of heaven is, You are also.

If Your kingdom has not entered me, truly neither shall I enter Your kingdom.
O immortal King, hear the utterance of my tongue; hear my song, the sole sacrifice of my tongue:

Blessed is the Kingdom of the Father and of the Son and of the Holy Spirit, Triradiate Life and Blessedness! Amen.

LXXXVI

Good will be with the just man.

Who ever searches for the grave of an unjust man? What purpose would it serve him? But everyone seeks the grave of the just man. They encircle it with a fence and erect a monument for it.

What purpose will it serve them? It is an acknowledgment by the world that the just man lives even after death, but that the unjust man perishes like a ripple in the water of the sea!

You are the justice of the just, O Living God. His justice is not to be found in the laws of men, laws which people write hastily but implement lazily. Your presence is his justice, and Your every breath -- is his new law.

A great just man has no old laws, nor does he care about laws written on paper. From the dawn of each morning he perceives You writing on his heart and his mind, and he reads.

Hundreds of ruffians and liars rise up against a just man and rejoice, after they clench his throat to silence him. But the ruffians and liars are admitting within themselves that all the wheels of the world have been clattering over them from dawn to dusk. In solitude, which is as distressing to those following their erring minds and ways as the dreadful Judgment Day, ruffians and liars admit that, to the extent that the world still exists, it exists only on account of the just -- on account of those just-minded people following the right way.

Who is a just man besides those who bear God within them? No one, Lord.

He who brings You into the world brings life into a shell of life, brings water into empty wells, and a song into muted throats.

As a cloud of dry smoke, without thunder or rain, is omnipotently dispersed to nothingness by the winds on high, so truly would this entire world be without God-bearers. The entire world is dry smoke, to which only a God-bearer can give thunder and rain, and which only a God-bearer can transform into a genuine cloud.

A cloud resembles a cloud, a man resembles a man, and a world resembles a world.

But one cloud is illusory dry smoke, while another is full of thunder and rain.

One man exists, while the other is nonexistent, even though one resembles the other. One world is, while the other is not, even though it appears as though they both exist.

Until You are born on earth, O Lord, the earth remains a nonexistent shadow; and all the beings on earth are nonexistent shadows.

Your birth is the entrance of electricity into a dry cloud.

Your words are the rain that makes a cloud a cloud.

Your miracles have created men out of vampires.

Your blood, and tears, and sweat have filled the empty shadow of the world with reality.

Good will always be with the just man. His grave will always be sought.

Indeed, the grave of the just man contains more power than the unjust living do. For the unjust are clouds of dry smoke.

Blessed is the nation which has its just!

LXXXVII

God-bearers, you are the salt of the earth and the light of the world.[130] If you lose your flavor and become dark, the world will be a shell of life, a snake's slough, which a serpent sheds amid the thorns.[131]

You contain the heavenly flame amid the ashes.[132] If you allow yourselves to die out, the world will be a pile of ashes beyond the gates of life.

Death-bearers babble about your life, because they have no life of their own.

Perjurers swear by your God, because they have no God of their own.

A liar justifies himself with your truth, because he has none of his own.

The world's wise men seek wisdom by a roundabout way and return to your wisdom, because there is no other.

Weaklings persecute you, because they fear your strength, and they themselves cannot take it away.

Cowards envy you for your courage, for there is nothing to encourage them.

---

[130] Cf. Matt. 5:13-14.
[131] Cf. Matt. *5:15-16* and 6:22-23.
[132] Cf. Mark 9:49-50, Luke 3:16 and 12:49.

Behold, the rich all beg from you, yet no one can give you anything. You are rich, for you have God. You are wealthy, for you are God-bearers.

Your soul is the cradle of the Living God. Your heart is His throne. Your mind is Mount Sinai, where He alone gives tablets of stone and speaks.[133]

Journey freely with God within you; you will not lose the way, and you will not be left without shelter. Enter with Him freely through the gates of the day, and the day will be yours. Enter with Him freely through the gates of the night, and the night will cringe with its specters, and will show you its wonders.

Do not sell your treasure, for the world cannot pay for it.[134]

Do not trade with the universe, for the universe can give nothing except itself. And its entirety is like paper compared to gold. It will burn up one day, and will be reduced to a handful of ashes.[135] Will it die? It is already dead, and has nothing without your spiritual treasure.

Space from one end to the other, cannot store your treasure.

Time, from one end to the other, cannot calculate your treasure.

The world persecutes you,[136] because you have peace, and it has none.

---

[133] Cf. Ex. 19 and 20.
[134] Cf. Matt. 13:44-46.
[135] Cf. 2 Pet. 3:10-12.
[136] Cf. Matt. 5:10-12 and John 15:20.

The world envies you, because you have wealth, and it is impoverished.

The world fears you, because you have power, and it is powerless.

The world hates you, because you have blessedness, and it is wretched.[137]

Do not spite the world, and do not add oil to the fire. For the whole world is ablaze with the flames of malice.

You have been isolated, you say? Are sepulchers really any kind of fellowship? One person alive in a cemetery is less alone than all the graves of the dead.

You are few in number, you say? But you are armed. Your adversaries are bound sepulchers.

The world is lifeless without you. You are the channels through which life pours into the world.

The world is joyless without you. Through you laughter is entering a prison.

Do not fatten your bodies, for to fatten is to fester. Do not pack mud onto your bones, for your bones will become sluggish and your souls will become thin.

Zealously keep the divine Bridegroom[138] within you, and beware lest you frighten Him away. He is truly as timorous as a bird, and will not impose Himself. At a

---

[137] Cf. Matt. 10:22 and John 15:18-25.
[138] Bridegroom Christ (Cf. Matt. 9:15 and 25:1-13, John 3:29).

single unseemly thought He flees from the mind. At a single filthy desire He flees from the heart.

Remember: if He abandons you, His last dug-out, the world will be a shell of life, a snake's slough, which a serpent sheds amid the thorns.

LXXXVIII

I raise my arms to You, my Shepherd, but my arms do not reach very far.
In vain does a sheep in a hole try to raise himself to the top; if the shepherd does not stoop down to help it, it will fall back in.

Your grace reaches further than the rays of the sun. Take hold of my hands, and lead me out of this dungeon. Just one ray of Your grace -- and I shall lift myself up on the wings of an eagle.

Beneath a stone grass is trying to grow, having become hunchbacked from seeking light and ashen faced from lack of light. Great is my joy as a mortal, when I lift the stone and see the grass straightening itself up and becoming green.

Was not Your joy even greater, Immortal Lord, when You lifted the stone that the world had rolled over my soul, hunchbacked and ashen-faced?
In vain do I gather wood into a pile to warm my soul, if You do not kindle it with fire from heaven.[139]

---

[139] Cf. Luke 12:49.

In vain do I run; if I am going the wrong way, my running is futile.

All my effort and my sweat is a sacrifice to You. If You are unwilling to accept it, I shall be like a mountain climber buried in snow on the mountain's peak.

For You do not look at the multitude of efforts but at the yearning of hearts.

What do you have to yearn for, my heart? Wherever the eye looks, it sees death. Whatever the hand touches it feels death.

Whatever you find, you also find the fear that you may lose it. Whatever you fall in love with fills you with the sorrow of its loss.

My restless thoughts, you push your way through my mind like drunkards at a fair, and you keep falling and dying like locusts on a highway. Everything that sent you into me will die, and not one of you will be saved from my grave, except those which have tied themselves to the Graveless, Undying Lord.

Truly, you entered a sepulcher when you entered me, and like gravediggers you are preparing my grave.

But when the trumpet, the long-tubed blaring trumpet, sounds in my soul, and heralds the coming of the Son of God![140] Then will all the mortal yearnings of my heart, and all the mortal thoughts of my mind be separated to the left, and the field of my heart and mind will be cleansed.[141]

---

[140] Cf. Matt. 24:31, 1 Cor. *15:52,* and 1 Thess. 4:16.
[141] Cf. Matt. 25:33 and 41.

And the Son of God will enter this field, and will level all the tombs you have prepared for me like molehills. And the Son of God will wash me and bathe me and make me fragrant with myrrh -- not for death but for life.[142]

I myself immured myself, O Lord, walling myself off from Your grace. And I did not dare to poke my head outside, for You are like a fearsome wind. I built shacks and shanties in my soul and was afraid that You would demolish them. But You have not demolished them in order to leave me homeless, but have done so in order to take me into a palace more spacious and radiant than the star-filled universe.

People rejected Your cornerstone, because it is too immense for their shacks and shanties.[143] Insane builders rejected it, because they do not know what to build on it. Being forgetful, they cannot remember that You are the builder, and that their whole job is not to interfere with You in Your work.

Your cornerstone is too immense, and giants are afraid to approach it. They say: "If we begin with this, when shall we finish?"

The wretches, how death frightens them off from every good beginning!

How time compels them to build one-day edifices!

Extend Your grace to me, grace which penetrates further than sunbeams, my Rich Lord, and I shall dare to stand beside the rejected stone.

---

[142] Cf. John. 9:39.
[143] Cf. Ps. 118:22, 23; Matt. 21:42.

Indeed, You are grace. Come down and lift me up.

Expel death and time from me and, together with You, I shall build what the earthly giants did not dare.

LXXXIX

The Son of God prophesied about the Temple on Moriah -- did He prophesy wrongly? Did stone remain on stone, and do worshippers still enter it today? Did He prophesy wrongly?[144]

A nation poured its whole soul into the walls of a single temple, and it remained empty and soulless. Whoever entrusts his whole soul to stone for protection and ceases to keep watch over it himself, will truly be as capricious in the world as the shadow of an aspen tree.

"We have built God a temple," say the capricious, "and we have paid off its debt. From now on we only have obligations to ourselves alone. We have given to God what is God's, now we shall give to ourselves what is ours."

You wretches, what need will God have for a temple, if you have no need for it? What will your temple mean to the One for whom a single grain of sand is not too fine and the star-filled universe is not too spacious. Can those who are themselves homeless really build a home for the Teacher of all builders?

---

[144] Cf. Matt. 24:1-2. The Temple in Jerusalem was destroyed by the Roman legions in 70 A.D. and has never been rebuilt since.

The Builder taught your ancestors and you yourselves to build Him temples, because you have need of them, not He.[145]

When you build for Him, you are building out of yourselves by means of Him. For earth can do nothing for Him without Him.

When you build the best for Him, you are setting an example for your soul, showing her what she should be building within herself.[146]

When you build for Him better than for your own body, you are setting an example for your soul, showing her that she should also be building herself a stronger, more sublime and radiant habitation than what the body needs and -- the body itself.[147]

When you build for Him, you are proving that your soul has not forgotten everything and has not reconciled herself to the shacks of the body.
You build Him expensive edifices, in order to remind your soul that she was intended for a royal palace, and not for hovels of clay.

You are not building a house for Him, but an image for your soul, a book and a reminder for your soul.

The Lord is overflowing with grace, and He comes down into your stone temples to meet with your souls.

But what will become of your temples, you wretches, if your soul does not heed and follow the example? If the

---

[145] Cf. Acts 7:48-50.
[146] CfICor.3:16-17.
[147] Cf. 1 Cor. 6:19.

domes of your temples are forever higher than your souls? If the width of your temples is forever wider than the narrowness of your souls? What will become of your temples?

If the candles in your temples of stone are forever brighter than the thoughts of your mind? If the myrrh and incense are forever more fragrant than the fragrance of your hearts? What will become of your temples?

If your altars are forever shining more brightly than all the shrines of your souls? If the splendor of your liturgies are forever more splendid than the splendors of your souls? If the resounding of the prayers in your temples finds more of an echo in the walls of stone than in your souls? What will become of your temples?

They will become the dead monuments of dead souls. And once they become this -- once they cease to be an example for the building up of the soul and become arrogance --truly, stone will not remain on stone. And you, wretches, will wander about as the shadows of those who built the temples and knew what they were building and why; and you will dance all over the world as capricious as the shadow of an aspen tree.

XC

Many in the world will stumble and fall because of Your Son, O Lord longer than time and more blessed than temporal generations.[148]

The princes of the people joined forces with robbers against the Most Pure Christ, as did the priests with false witnesses and the learned with the demented.

Oh how majestic He is in His aloneness and in the purity of His way!

The scribes, who had spent their lifetime interpreting the law of God, now all rose up in unison not only to judge, but to put a man to death.

The leaders of the people, who wore the written law from Sinai on their breast, around their waist and on their temples, forgot the several thousand years of their being trained in justice, and like ravenous wolves they ran after the Man of peace and goodness to tear Him apart.

The merchants closed their shops and drew their daggers to kill Him.

The elders, decorated with countless external reminders of God's miracles among their people, but with no internal ones, dragged themselves from their hearths to join in the kill.

---

[148] Cf. Matt. 26:31-33, 1 Cor. 1:23, 1 Peter 2:7-8.

The youths, who tend to revel whenever their elders urge them to do something wicked, went out with sticks and stones to commit murder before sitting down for the Passover and glorifying God.

Even the women rose up for blood, and led their children forth, so that even the children could assist in a national deed.

Cutthroats and ruffians, who on other days would have been slithering through the shadows and alley-ways, now became leaders to the leaders and princes to the princes.

For the criminals in prison came the day of liberation, for the people needed them to teach them how to kill a man.[149]

All the visitors [in Jerusalem] who had come to the city for the feast in order to bow down to Heaven and petition God, turned their backs on the Temple and, together with their hosts and innkeepers, rushed to seek the blood of a righteous man.

The priests forgot the Temple and set out with their sacrificial knives, in order to save the people from God.

The lame and the crippled raised their crutches and the blind raised their begging-bowls -- as their only weapons to help kill the healer.

Thus did a nation of sinners rise up, as unanimously as grass, to kill God. And the dagger that they swung against God slipped, and they stabbed themselves in the heart.

---

[149] Cf. Matt. 27:15-26.

Grant that I not also fall, O dearest Lord!

Open the eyes of my soul, so that I may see and learn from the fate of sinners.

May my feet not follow those, who march against You.

May I never in any way raise a stone at You and slay myself forever.

Grant that I not also fall, O dearest Lord.

XCI

The blood of a righteous man is the only writing on earth that cannot be erased.

Did you kill the Christ, you desperate people, as you had hoped? Or does His blood even today burn on your heads?[150]

Proclaim with your roar, O sea, to all the ends of the earth:

The blood of the righteous burns on the head for a hundred generations.[151]

Crisscross from the east to the west, O thunder, and inscribe it clearly even for the blind: People can do no

---

[150] Cf. Matt. 27:25.
[151] Cf. Matt. 23:29-36.

evil to one who is righteous, and may this evil not come crashing down twice as hard onto their own heads![152]

For a stone cast at a righteous man has been thrown up high, and as it falls from the heights it becomes all the heavier.

The stones of Jerusalem, which today lie around all scattered, cry out and exclaim to the human race, a forgetful race, what became of a slain righteous man and what became of those who slew him!

I saw a dog burn its tongue on steaming hot porridge once, and it has never again approached even cold porridge. And I see people day after day burning themselves with the blood of the righteous, and yet they never avoid it.

O you who are more insane than the insane, are you not at all ashamed to have repeated a lesson that even a dog learned the first time?

It is better for a bloodthirsty nation to disappear rather than a single righteous man. For heaven does not ask how much blood is spilled, but whose blood is spilled.[153]

If all the nations were to rise up against one righteous man, they would not be able to do him any harm. They can only be his escort to the grave. But he will escort them after the grave.[154]

---

[152] Cf. 1 Peter 3:13-14.
[153] Cf. Ps. 116:15.
[154] Cf. Luke 12:4-5.

Truly, the righteous man inflicts punishment with his mercifulness before the grave and with his righteousness after the grave.

Do not ensure belongings for your children, you who have joined in shedding the blood of a righteous man. Indeed, all your belongings will be lost to them except for the blood that you spilled.

And it will not be the righteous man who will hurl a curse on you, but your own children, when they will have eaten the bitter bread of slaves.[155]

God conceals Himself in the rags of the righteous. Woe to you, if those rags disturb you, and consequently you also despise the one clad in those rags.

You were raised up on the cross, O Christ our God, not in order to manifest Your powerlessness over the world, but in order to manifest the world's powerlessness over You.

Like shadows that beat upon a boulder in the moonlight, so also are those nations powerless, who strike at You.

O Lord, the solace of the righteous and the courage of the martyrs, have mercy on us and save us.

---

[155] Cf. Ex. 34:7 and Num. 14:18.

XCII

My Lord is the One who resurrects. He resurrects the dead from morning until dusk, and from dusk until dawn.[156]

What the morning buries, the Lord brings to life in the evening; and what the evening buries, the Lord brings to life in the morning.

What work is more fitting for the living God than to resurrect the dead into life?

Let others believe in the God who brings men to trial and judges them.

I shall cling to the God who resurrects the dead.

Let others believe in the God, who does not even draw near to the living when they call upon Him.

I shall worship the God, who holds His cupped ear even at cemeteries and listens, to hear whether anyone is crying out for resurrection or for the One who resurrects.

The gravediggers dig graves and are silent. The Lord opens graves and shouts.[157]

---

[156] "Jesus said... 'I *am* the resurrection and the life. He who believes in Me, though he may die, he shall live'" (John 11:25).
[157] Cf. John 5:24-30 and 1 Thess. 4:13-17.

A mother places her daughter in a grave, the Lord takes her out of the grave; the Lord is a better mother than the mother.

A father covers his son with soil, the Lord uncovers him. The Lord is a better father than the father.

A brother buries his brother, the Lord resurrects him. The Lord is a better brother than the brother.

The Lord has neither tears nor smiles for the dead. His whole heart belongs to the living.

The world mourns for their kindred in the cemeteries, the Lord seeks His own with a song and awakens them.

Resurrect my soul, O Lord, so that my body might also be resurrected. Dwell in my soul, and my body will become Your temple.[158]

My neighbors ask with anxiety whether this body of ours will be resurrected.
If you have denied yourself once and for all, and no longer live for yourself, then your body is already being resurrected.[159]

If your body is a temple of the Most High God, then the One who resurrects is within you, and your resurrection is already being accomplished.

Our body changes with age, throughout our lifetime we have called many bodies our own. Which of them will be resurrected?

---

[158] Cf. 1 Cor. 6:19.
[159] Cf. Gal. 2:20, Rom 6:3-11, and Col. 2:12.

Perhaps none of them. But you can be certain that if you have had a body which expresses the Word of God clearly, it will be resurrected.[160]

My Lord who resurrects, does not resurrect death, because death was never alive.

You are the One who resurrects and You are the resurrection, for You are life.[161]

Only the seed which contains You is resurrected, and that seed which is of You.[162]

You will only bring to life that soul which now lives by You and not by the world.

You will only preserve that body, which has begun to be filled with the Holy Spirit during this time.[163]

That which is of the Living God in the graves, will be resurrected into life.
No one can resurrect the dead except the Lord, and no one can rise from the dead except the Lord.

For He is in His holy people. Truly, He is in His living people, both in the grave and out of the grave.

---

[160] Cf. 1 Cor. 15:35-57.
[161] Cf. John 11:25.
[162] Cf. John 12:24.
[163] Cf. Phil. 3:10-11, 20-21.

XCIII

The One wished for has come, and will come again, and yet you ask: "Who will prove to us that He is God?"

I shall ask you, somber brethren, and you respond to what I ask: "If you were to have God come to earth, in what form would you wish to see Him?"

"We should wish to see Him as a man, fairer than all the sons of men, mightier than all the sons of men in word and mightier than all the sons of men in deed. We should wish to see Him as an exceedingly handsome prince; not haughty but as meek as a lamb; someone who would come under our roofs, eat and drink with us, and share everything in common with us except our weakness and sin."

Then I tell you: "You yourselves have already proven that God was among us."

"We should wish to see Him as a man, although He can reveal Himself in any fleshly form. When He speaks, He should speak mightily, as no man has ever spoken. When He walks through this world, He should not walk as a hireling and a slave but as a Lord. Water and winds should listen to Him, people should follow Him, evil spirits should flee from Him. He should be of assistance to people every day: comforting those who mourn, healing the sick, resurrecting the dead. We should wish Him to be this sort of God among us."

Then I tell you: "You yourselves have proven that God was among us."

"We should wish for Him to come to us not as a king with a wealth that perishes, with an army that vanishes, or with a luster that tarnishes -- not as a king but as One greater than kings. And we should wish for Him to come to us not as an ordinary prophet, but rather as the One who was prophesied from the beginning of time, as One who would dare to say that He is older than time, as One who would prophesy to us what will happen at the end of time and after the end of time. And we should wish for Him to come to us not as a priest but as a high priest, in whom all three appear together, God, priest, and sacrifice. This is how we should wish for God to manifest Himself among us."

Then I tell you: "You yourselves have proven that God was among us."

"We should wish for Him to come and go quickly, for we should not be able to endure Him for long. Once He were to come, however, we should wish for His word to reverberate throughout time and space, never ending or stopping; and we should wish. for the earth to be kindled by His steps and to burn with heavenly fire, as long as the earth lasts."

Then I tell you: "You yourselves have proven that God was among us."
The One wished for came among men in whatever way men could have wished, and even better still, and mightier still, and fairer still, and even so, even then people said: "Who will prove to us that this is God?"

The One wished for will come again, my soul. Like a fiery dragon He will fly up to you and, if you do not recognize Him, He will fly away, and truly you will see Him no more. Arise, my soul, do not sleep but keep watch. Implant in yourself the image of the One wished for, what He is like, so that you may recognize Him when He comes.

Let the images of all worlds leave you, my soul, and let His image fill you entirely, from east to west, from north to south --so that you may recognize Him when He comes.

For He will come and go like a fiery dragon, and yet you will be dozing and saying: "Who will prove to us...?"

If you do not prove it to yourself, no one will ever prove it to you.

If your everlasting life does not prove Him to you, your everlasting death will.

XCIV

In the valley of tears You brought dead bones to life, O Divine Son.[164]
Let the prophet rejoice, for You fulfilled his prophecy.

All the strength, all the beauty, and all the wisdom, for which the whole of mankind has been yearning from the beginning, is found in You, the Ultimate Man.

All the food of life and all the drink of life, by means of which the living have been living from one end of time to the other, are found in You, the Ultimate Man.

Through You the Triradiate Ray dared to project itself into the darkness of death and the shadow of

---

[164] Cf. Ezek. 37:1-14.

nonexistence. Beneficence was in that Ray and, like every benefaction, it was abused. Therefore the Ray withdrew, and the darkness of death and the shadow of nonexistence reigned.

Then You came with a new Ray and a new beneficence. And those who accepted You began to shine like newly kindled suns.[165]

But those who did not accept You, remained dead bones in the valley to an even greater degree.

You opened up a bakery for the hungry and a tavern for the thirsty, and You invite all those who hunger and thirst to eat and drink and to be living beings.

Whoever desires life, must nourish himself with life. Whoever surrenders himself to death, nourishes himself with death, and is not found among the living.

You brought God to us in the vale of torments; You brought God to us, not to show Him to us as an image (the dancing of images devours our soul), but as bread for us to eat and thereby come back to life.[166] We nourished ourselves with images and died. Truly, all those things which mortals eat and drink are images, that do not nourish or quench thirst or give life, unless God enters into them.

Let my soul eat God, and she will be crowned with everlasting life.

Let my mind eat God, and it will be crowned with everlasting wisdom.

---

[165] Cf. John 1:1-18, Phil. 2:15, Eph. 5:8-14.
[166] Cf. John 6:32-59.

Let my heart eat God, and it will be crowned with everlasting joy.

Let my body eat God, and it will be resurrected from the dead.

Let all people eat God, and they will return home, they will return to the Ultimate Man.

You have no grave among us. Earth contains only earth. Sepulchers are buried in graves, and remain in them.

O Prince of the Holy Triad and King of all creatures, who at Your word began to breathe and see, nourish me with Your bread, and quench my thirst with Your drink.

Lest my body disintegrate, and my soul box her way through Hades as a fleshless shadow, filled with absurd perceptions, filled with fleshly desires, filled with fright and frightful images.

Lest I lose, O Lord, both bodies: my earthly body, which is closer to perishing than the autumn grass, and my heavenly body, which the spirit is waiting to weave and make ready for eternity.

Lest I lose, O Lord, both spirits: my earthly spirit, which has betrothed itself to death by being wedded to earth, and my heavenly spirit, which I have not received within me to bring its eternity into me.

Lest I lose, O Lord, both lives: my earthly life, which resembles life, and my heavenly life, which is life.

Come closer to me, and closer still, O Heavenly Bread, and do not resist my mouth.

Come closer to me, and closer still, O Heavenly Drink, and do not avoid my lips.

O All-Holy Trinity, bring Your lantern into my night and scare away the stranger, who is blocking me from You.

XCV

Children and saints cling to You, O Lord, the rest rebel against You.
Children and saints are the boundary between the Kingdom of existence and the shadow of nonexistence.[167]

Guardians call themselves parents and cast Your children off crags into chasms.

Guardians presume that they are parents, and so they direct Your children as though they were their own property. Truly, they are directing nothing but aberrations and disruptions.

The children, whom you guardians have abducted, belong to another, and you will answer for theft and banditry.

You own neither the life that is in you, nor the life for which you served as a channel. Everything belongs to

---

[167] Cf. Matt. 18:2-5.

another, except for the wickedness within you, and you will answer for theft and banditry.

You will answer for theft, because you have been calling those who belong to another, your own; and you will answer for banditry, because you have mutilated and butchered those who belong to another.

On earth there are only guardians; and this is a very great honor.
You have been entrusted with the guardianship of the most precious treasure that God has. And this is a very great honor.

One, who was never even born and was never entrusted with the guardianship of anything, will be more blessed than you, if your guardianship is an abomination and a mortification of souls.[168]

Why do you rejoice in children, unless you intend to keep watch over them as though they were angels from heaven? Why do you grieve for them, when they leave you early and flee to the angels in heaven? You were rejoicing in what belongs to another, and you are grieving for what belongs to another.

Do not care only about keeping the bodies of your children safe, for even foxes do the same for their foxling. Hut care about God in your children. Once God is cared for He will take care of all the rest. And what you have been accumulating for your children so strenuously, He will effortlessly gather for them quickly and easily.[169]

---

[168] Cf. Matt. 18:6.
[169] Cf. Matt. 6:33.

Do not drive God out of your children, for you will deprive them of their peace, their happiness, their health, and their prosperity.

Even if you leave the entire world to those whom God has left, you will have left it to starving people, who will devour it all and still die of hunger.

Do not ensure a piece of bread for your children, but a piece of the soul and the conscience. Your children will be ensured and you will be blessed in two worlds.

Care for this property of another better than your own, and your reward will be immense.

Royal children have been entrusted to your guardianship. Truly, the King will give no small reward to those who guard His princely progeny, and have not erased the Father's name from those children's memory.

Through children the King is looking at you with amazement, and is awaiting your responses. If your responses are deathful, you will be taking care of corpses.

Children and saints cling to You, my Lord, the rest rebel against You. Children and saints are Your way of testing the world.

Be careful, my soul, be careful and make no mistake.

XCVI

Every creature frightened me when I was a child; but since the time I grew up I have felt compassion for every creature.

Every creature seemed to me to be stronger than me while I was a child. Now I feel stronger than everything, and I feel compassion for everything.
For I learned to stand beside You, my Lord, who are surrounded by immortal hosts like a mountain covered with pines. And I have been growing out of You, like a tree out of a mountain.

While I was a child, I took each creature to be my teacher and spent some time with each of them. And I learned about infirmity and death and crying out to You.

I searched for the strongest creature, so that I could grab hold of it and save myself from change and fluctuation. But my eyes never did see it, nor did my ears ever hear it, nor did my feet ever stumble upon it. Time raises all its children in order to wrestle with them, and in order to bend them as a joke and to snap them in two and tear them out by the roots as it laughs at the horror and terror of mortals.

I grabbed hold of a flower and said: "In beauty it is stronger than I am." But when autumn arrived, the flower died before my eyes, and I could do nothing to help it. So I turned away with tears and grabbed hold of tall trees.

But with the passage of time, the trees were torn out by the roots, and fell to the ground like vanquished soldiers, and I turned away with tears, and grabbed hold of stone. "It is stronger than me," I said, "with it I am secure." But with the passage of time the stone crumbled to dust before my eyes, and the wind carried it off and I turned away with tears and latched onto the stars. "The stars are stronger than anything," I said, "I shall cling to them and shall not fall."

But after I embraced the stars and began to converse with them in secret whispers, I heard the moaning of the dying, and I turned away with tears and latched onto people. "People strut erectly and freely," I said, "there is strength in them; I shall cling to them lest I fall."

But with the passage of time I saw even the strongest among men helplessly skidding on the ice of time into the soundless abyss, and they left me solitary.

In an anxious sweat I contemplated the universe in its entirety and said: "You are stronger than everything. I shall cling to you. Keep me from skidding into the soundless abyss." And I obtained this response: "This evening I too am sinking into the soundless abyss, and tomorrow there will be another universe in my place. In vain do you tie yourself to me, for I am your feeble fellow wayfarer."

Again I turned to people, to the wisest among the sons of men, and I asked for their counsel. But they quarreled as they gave me answers, until death waved its hand and brought stillness into the midst of the squabblers.

Again I turned to people, to the happiest among the sons of men, and asked for their opinion. (As though any opinion could be given by those who think by means of flesh!) But they took me as a joke for their amusement, until death raised its staff and covered their tongues with mold.

Again I turned to people, to those who begot me and brought me among creatures, and I asked them. Their wrinkled faces began to turn pale; their eyes filled with tears; and they started to stammer: "In ignorance we were begotten, in ignorance we begot you, and our ignorance we share with you."

Again I turned to people, to my friends and I said: "What do you think, my friends?" But they kept a long silence, until with shame and without lifting their eyes they began to mutter: "For a long time we have been preparing to ask you what you think."

And when I knocked on the very last door to ask my question, the door opened and I saw a dead man being carried out.

When there were no more doors to knock on, even my tears ceased, and a searing fear stuck its claws into my bones.

One last tear was still to be found, and it rolled its way down to the bottom of my soul. And behold, some unknown door, which that final tear struck, opened, and then You appeared, my King and my Father, all surrounded by immortal hosts like a pine-covered mountain engulfed in un scorching flame.

And light began to dance like the many sounds of a harp, and I heard a voice saying: "I am the One whom you seek. Cling to Me. My name is: **I AM.**"

XCVII

Your visit, my Power, brings powers to every creature.

You pour oil into each of them as into empty lamps, and they begin to burn.
Blessed is he who receives You into his own emptiness; he will be filled and will burn.

When there is no oil, the wick burns with smoke and a sooty odor.

People used to burn before Your visit, but this was not You who would burn, but the wick with its smoke and sooty odor.

When You came to visit the earth, You filled all the lamps with oil and the oil began to burn, without the smoke and the sooty odor.

However the ignorant see no difference, but say: "There was burning before, and there is burning now."

The ignorant see no difference between the burning of an empty lamp and the burning of a full lamp.

O you ignorant people, when earth burns with its own fire, this is a wick that is burning and not oil, and it burns with smoke and a sooty odor.

When earthen vessels are filled with heavenly oil, the oil burns, and its burning is with flame and light, but without smoke and the sooty odor.

Indeed, You are not like ordinary visitors, who come to take. You did not come in order to come and go like ordinary visitors, nor to come and take, but rather you came in order to leave something behind -- truly, in order to fill everything and leave it full!

You brim with blessings, O Lord, and every creature is filled with might and power, after You have come to visit.

Water, which used to be able to wash only the body, obtained the power to baptize the soul -- in Your name, O Lord![170]

Oil, which used to be able to glisten only on a healthy face, obtained the power to give strength to the sick -- in Your name, O Lord![171]

Bread, which used to be able only to pile up ashes upon ashes within a man, obtained the power to nourish life with Your life -- in Your name, O Lord![172]

The springs have been imbued with strength, and the grasses of the field have ripened with life -- in Your name, O Lord!

Words have become a cure, and signs have become a defense -- in Your name, O Lord![173]

The dead have begun to take the infirmities of the living upon themselves and the living have begun to converse

---

[170] Cf. John 3:5-6.
[171] Cf. James 5:14.
[172] Cf. John 6:32-59.
[173] The name of Christ and the sign of the Cross.

with the dead as with the living -- in Your name, O Lord![174]

Tombs, out of which only stench used to seep, have begun to pour forth myrrh, and the dens of wild beasts have become caves for penitents -- in Your name, O Lord![175]

Before Your visit, O Lord, everything was smokier than a burning wick, and everything was frailer than a cobweb.

Will the ignorant open their eyes and see the difference? For all who are ignorant I kneel and pray before You, O Lord Almighty: Open their eyes, so that they may see the difference.

So that they may see the difference and open their empty lamps, for You to fill them.

So that they may not be forever choking in the smoke and sooty odor, O Heavenly Oil of my lamp.

For all who are ignorant I kneel and pray before You, O Holy Life-creating Spirit.

Blow like a gale and shake up the souls of the ignorant, so that they may wake up and experience the hour of Your visitation.

---

[174] I.e., the relics of the saints effecting cures and the living praying to the saints.

[175] I.e., the wonderworking myrrh that has flowed out from the reliquaries of such saints as St. Demetrius and St. Simeon of Serbia; the caves in the wilderness being occupied by hermits and monastics.

So that they may repent and kneel down with me and exclaim: "How new earth becomes, after You visit it, O Majestic and Awesome God!"

XCVIII

I am a book inscribed both inside and out, and sealed with seven seals.[176] My neighbors sound out the letters but cannot pronounce my name.

My neighbors, how then will you read the name of the Lord, who has cleansed me from the mire, if you cannot pronounce my name?

I am Your book, my Lord and King, I am Your writing both inside and out. Only the world smears me with its illiterate hand, and I become unclear and illegible.

I am Your book, my Lord and King, and the seals, with which You sealed me as Your sacred scripture, are Yours.

Beneath each seal is concealed one of the gifts of the Holy Spirit,[177] one of the gifts of the everlasting life of the Heavenly Triad. Who will open what God has sealed --who can except God alone?

---

[176] Cf. Rev. 5:1.

[177] The seven gifts of the Holy Spirit are: wisdom, understanding, counsel, spiritual strength, spiritual knowledge, true godliness and the fear of God.

My neighbors say to me: "You are inscribed all over by the hand of the world, and all the gifts within you are gifts of the world, and yet you are a holy book?"

Thus do the illiterate read me, and I feel that they do not know my name.

Truly, the world has scrawled much on my heart with its clumsy hand. And the world has stuffed many unsolicited gifts into my heart.

Nevertheless, even when I erase all the world's scrawling from my heart and throw out all the worldly gifts from my heart, I am not throwing my heart out of myself nor am I leaving it empty.

Moreover, when I erase all the scrawling of the world on my mind and throw out all the worldly gifts from my mind, I am not throwing my mind out of myself, nor am I leaving it empty.

And I know, that my spirit has written on my body, and my body has written on my spirit. Indeed, even if I erase all the writing of my spirit on my body, and all the writing of my body on my spirit, I shall nevertheless not remain an uninscribed book.

When I throw the entire world out of myself, again I see within myself a book sealed with seven seals. This is Your book, O Lord. This is the scripture of my Lord. Who can unseal God's book except God alone?

Whoever acknowledges You as the Father, You acknowledge as a son, and for a son You open the book and read to him the mysteries. You break seal after seal, and read to him the mysteries.

In vain do people read me, they will not be reading me. They will be reading only what the world has inscribed on me and in me. But their eyes cannot read beneath the seals.

There are not many words in this book, but each word is as fiery as flame and as long as immortality, and is more pleasurable than all the pleasures of this world.

Seven words -- seven spirits and seven lives, three above and three below, indivisibly connected in the center to one undying flame.

The sacred masculinity of heaven and the virginal femininity of earth, a flame girded with an immaculate sash, adorned with seven stars.

But who dares to cast a pearl before those who feed on rotting apples? Who dares to read Your mysteries to those who are literate only when it comes to the fat letters of the world?

An invisible hand is trying to write everywhere throughout the world, but the world keeps vying and striving with its own deathful hand to write -- lethal letters.

O Lord All-merciful, look upon those who look upon You, and guide their hand, so that, when they write, they may write Your name on themselves both inside and Out.

O my God All-wise, direct the eyes of Your elect to the seals of Your book, so that they may anticipate with prayer and read with understanding, once You quietly and gently break the seals of the mysteries

XCIX

Few have listened, O Lord, and yet there are those who believe.

Few are those, who fix their eyes on their Lord and follow His gaze.

I am searching for those who have listened, my Lord, and I share my joy with them. I tell them about Your ways and Your wisdom, and they confirm what I relate. And we multiply our joy and -- share it.

I listen to the tale of those who have listened, how You removed the stumbling blocks before their feet, and I add my own story, and our room is filled with heaven.

We strew all the events that have happened to us onto the fine sieve of Your law, and we call the chaff that falls out Yours, and we call the pure grain that remains Yours.

We count all pains, all tears and all sufferings endured for the sake of Your name, as our gain.

"What good is our faith from Sunday to Sunday," we say, "If it does not keep us in sight of our Master every day?"

There are those who believe, O Lord our God, yet those who listen are few.

To whom shall I listen, if not to the Most Mighty? Will those who are knocked down lift me up, and will mortals strengthen me?

To whom shall I listen, if not to the Most Wise? Will the untaught teach me, and will ignoramuses show me the truth?

To whom shall I listen if not to the Most Holy? Will sinners protect me, and will bloodshedders save my soul?

What would one call a man who is lost, were he to spy a fire in the darkness of night and not set his course toward that fire?

And what would one call a boatman who sees a light on the pier, and steers his boat away?

Those who believe but do not listen to You could be called the same name.

You felt the barb of my own refusal to listen, my love, forgive me!

Ever since Your love wounded me, shame has roasted me from the memory of my heedlessness.

I had been adorned with faith in You, as with flowers, but I used to walk my own ways, unaware that Your love was accompanying my every step.

Now my eyes have been opened to Your love. You have wounded me severely, and the wound roasts me like fire.

Now I see, that Your love has been accompanying me on all the steep hillsides and crossroads of my life. I look into the past and I see only two things: Your love and my refusal to listen. You have wounded me severely, and the wound roasts me like fire.

To whom shall I confess my sin except to You, against whom I have sinned?

Why should I confess to those who refuse to listen to You, to those who would say: "You did not sin much, for we have also done likewise?" They would justify my sin by their own sin, and they would give me no solace.

They would make their own sin the criterion of justice between You and me, and would adjudge justice to be on the side of the sinner.

You have wounded me severely with Your love, and the wound roasts me like fire. Again Your mercy is immeasurable, and You have opened my eyes before I have died.

Forgive me, O Lord, and command Your servant!

How even now You meekly look and command, as though I had never sinned against You at all!

Command, O Master, and lash with a whip, and help my conscience to flagellate me.

You have wounded me severely, and the wound roasts me like fire. Let it be so. Let it roast me like three fires, until I become accustomed to be as attentive as an angel in heaven.

Until my attentiveness to Your will, O Lord, becomes the sole pleasure of my days and nights, as long as I live.

C

Accept the sacrifice of my words, my Father -- accept the babbling of a penitent child, my Father!

Correct my words with Your truth, and accept them on the footstool of Your feet.

Cense my sacrifice with the fragrant incense of a saint's prayer and do not reject it, O Triradiate Master of worlds.

The ranks of angels offer You a more eloquent sacrifice, but their words stream to them from You, and return to You, untainted by the repulsiveness of darkness and not throttled in the throat by sin.

I am poor, and I have nothing else to offer on Your sacrificial altar except these words.

Even if I were to offer up creatures to You, I would be offering up words. For what are creatures except words. You have filled the entire universe with tongues, which are flames when they lift up praise to You and water -- when they whisper Your praises to themselves.

Even if I were to offer up a lamb to You, I would be offering You a word.

Even if I were to offer up a bird to You, I would be offering You a word.

Why should I offer up someone else's word to my Lord, why someone else's and not my own?

Who has made me master over someone else's life and someone else's song, over someone else's flame and someone else's sacrifice; who?

My words are my life and my song, my flame and my sacrifice. I have taken from what is Yours and am offering it up to You -- accept it and do not reject it, O Mother plenteous in lovingkindness.

I have picked a handful of wheat out of a field of tares, accept even a single kernel of wheat out of my handful and You will make me happy.[178]

From a single kernel You can bake bread, enough for nations.

Accept my mite, O Son Who Resurrects, accept and do not reject the mite of a pauper.[179]

Accept my sacrifice not for my sake but for the sake of someone who is even more impoverished than I; is there such a person?

Someone who does not even have what I do, for his sake accept my sacrifice; does such a person exist?

The world squeezed me like an accordion, scarcely did I take a breath and I moaned. Let Your angels give melody to my moaning and let them offer it up before You, my love.

---

[178] Cf. Matt. 13:24-3O.
[179] Cf. Mark 12:41-44.

I remind myself of all the blessings You have bestowed on me during my lifetime, my unfailing Companion, and I am offering up to You a gift in return from myself.

I am not offering up to You my entire self, for I am not entirely worthy to burn on Your most pure sacrificial altar. I cannot offer as a sacrifice to the Immortal One what is intended for death and corruption.

I offer up to You only that which has grown within me under Your light, that which was saved in me by Your Word.

Accept the sacrifice of my words, O Triune Bouquet of Flowers; accept the babbling of a new-born child.

When the choirs of angels begin to sing around Your throne, when the archangels' trumpets begin to blare, when Your martyrs begin to weep for joy, and Your saints begin to sob their prayers for the salvation of the Church on earth, do not despise the sacrifice of my words, O Lord my God.
Do not mishear, but hear.

I pray to You and bow down to You, now and throughout all time, and throughout all eternity. Amen.

Written at Lake Ohrid 1921-1922.

GLOSSARY

Allah -- The Moslem name of the Supreme Being.

Angels - the spiritual "messengers" of God. In the "Celestial Hierarchy" of the early Church Father, Dionysius the Pseudo-Areopagite (c. 500 A.D.), the angels are arranged in three hierarchies containing three choirs each, in the order of Seraphim, Cherubim and Thrones; Dominlons, Powers, and Authorities; Principalities, Archangels and Angels.

Authorities -- see "Angels".

Brahma -- in Hindu theology, originally the absolute, self- existent, eternal essence or spirit of the universe, the source of all things, the object of the loftiest philosophical adoration -- later it became personified as the first person in the Hindu trinity with Vishnu (redeemer) and Siva (destroyer). Brahmana is represented by a red figure with four heads and four arms.

Buddha -- (Sanskrit = the enlightened one) tide given the founder of Buddhism, Siddhartha Gautama (c. 563-c.483 B.C.). His father was a king of the warrior caste and raised his son in great luxury, but at the age of 29, Siddhartha renounced the world to become a wandering ascetic and search for a solution to the problems of death and human suffering. After six years of spiritual discipline, he achieved supreme enlightenment at the age of 35. He spent the rest of his life teaching his doctrines and establishing a community of monks to continue his work.

Cain -- in the Bible, the oldest son of Adam and Eve: he killed his brother, Abel (cf. Gen. 4).

Christology -- the study of the person of Christ, and in particular of the union in Him of the divine and human natures.

Dominions -- see "Angels."

empirical-- relying or based on experiments or experience; as in, the *empirical* method.

Fall -- *77:e Fall of Man* or *the Fall* is, in Christian theology, the lapse of the human race from a state of innocence into one of innate sinfulness and original sin, owing to the disobedience of Adam and Eve in the Garden of Eden, when they ate the fruit of the tree of the knowledge of good and evil. (Cf. Genesis, ch. 2 and 3).

Godhead -- divinity, godhood, the state or quality of being God; also, God Himself. *Triune Godhead:* the Holy Trinity as three Persons yet one Deity.

God-man -- (Serbian *Bogochovek,* Greek *Theanthropos).* In Orthodox Christian theology this term denotes the person of Jesus Christ, who possesses both a divine nature (from God the Father) and a human nature (from His mother, the Virgin Mary).

Herod -- ruled as king at the time of Christ's birth, according to Matt. 2:1-18 (cf. Luke 1:5). His infamous ruthlessness in defending his throne against any threat accounts for the story of the massacre of Bethiehem's innocent infants (cf. Matt. 2:16-17). Hindu -- any member of those peoples of India who speak languages derived from the Indic branch of Indo-European. Also an adherent of Hinduism.

hypostasis -- in Christian theology, (1) originally, the unique essence or nature of the Godhead and, therefore, of the three persons of the Trinity; (2) any of the three persons of the Trinity; (3) the personality of Christ as distinguished from His two natures, human and divine. (plural: *hypostases).*

I AM -- the first part of the formula by which God identified Himself to Moses on Mount Sinai: "I am who I am" = Yahweh or, as the name appears m the King James Version, "Jehovah." (See Ex. 3:14). Thus Jesus answered the Jews (in John *8:58):* "Before Abraham was, I AM." See also the *One who Is.*

imam -- a Moslem priest who performs the regular service of the mosque.

Karma -- (Sanskrit: a deed, act) in Buddhism and Hinduism, the totality of a person's actions in one of the successive states (through reincarnation) of his existence, thought of as determining his fate in the next. Loosely: fate or destiny.

Kismet -- Turkish word (qismet) for doom, appointed lot, fate, or predetermined fortune.

knowledge, tree of-- See: tree of knowledge.

Krishna -- A very popular deity in Hinduism, the eighth avatar, or incarnation, of Vishnu.

Lao-tse (or Lao-tsu) -- A sixth-century B.C. Chinese philosopher and founder of Taoism.

Life, Tree of-- See Tree of Life.

Logos -- See *Word of God.*

lotus position -- in yoga, an erect sitting posture with the legs crossed and with each foot, Sole upturned, resting on the upper thigh of the opposite leg.

minaret -- a high slender tower attached to a Moslem mosque, with one or more projecting balconies, from which a muezzin, or crier, calls the people to prayer.

Moriah -- the rocky hill in Jerusalem where Solomon built the Jewish Temple (2 Chron. 3:1).

muezzin -- in Moslem regions, a crier in a minaret or other lofty place who calls the people to prayer at the proper hours.

nirvana -- in Buddhism, the state of perfect blessedness achieved by the extinction of individual existence and by the absorption of the soul into the supreme spirit, or by the extinction of all desires and passions.

Nous -- (Greek) In philosophy, mind, understanding, intellect, reason; in theology and patristic literature, the Son of God is sometimes referred to as the *Nous* of God the Father.

One Who Is, the -- the name by which God identified Himself to Moses on Mt. Sinai (Ex. 3:14), also translated as "I am Who I am" (see: I AM). In Hebrew this name is "Yahweh" and appears in the King James Version as "Jehovah." In the Septuagint Greek version of the Old Testament the divine epithet is translated by three letters which often appear in the cruciform halo behind Christ's head in Orthodox iconography.

Powers -- see "Angels."

Principalities -- see "Angels."

Rishis -- in Hindu legend it is said that in ancient days seven Wise Men, or *Rishis,* acquired, by penance and meditation, complete knowledge of all things. Later applied to the sages and saints of India, both Hindu and Buddhist, who were viewed as their avatars through reincarnation.

Sadducees -- A Jewish politico-religious sect, opposed to the Pharisees. Though never popular, they stood for the interests of the priestly aristocracy and the rich, and exercised great political influence at the time of Christ. They rejected belief in an afterlife and the resurrection, and took a leading part against Christ in collaboration with the Romans. They also at tacked Christ's Apostles for proclaiming His resurrection. They disappear from history after the destruction of Jerusalem by Rome in 70 A.D.

scribes -- (as used here:) the teachers or doctors of the Old Testament Jewish law who, together with the Pharisees, rigidly insisted on meticulous external adherence to that law and frequently criticized and condemned Christ for following the spirit, rather than the letter, of the law.

slava -- (Serbian word meaning "glory") in Serbian Orthodox religious tradition, the rites performed with special bread *(kolach)* and wine in order to glorify one's patron saint on his feast day, usually accompanied by a sumptuous meal and large numbers of guests in one's home.

Tao -- (see Taoism).

Taoism -- A Chinese philosophical system (which later evolved into a religion) deriving chiefly from writings ascribed to Lao-tse (6th cent. B.C.). According to its teaching, man's ideal state of freedom from desire and of effortless simplicity is achieved by following the Tao (Chinese = "way"), the spontaneous, creative functioning of the universe.

Thrones -- see "Angels."

tree of knowledge -- in the Bible, the tree whose fruit Adam and Eve tasted in disobedience to God. See Genesis, ch. 2 and 3. Also referred to as *the tree of the knowledge of good and evil.*

Tree of Life -- in the Bible, a tree in the Garden of Eden bearing fruit which, if eaten, gave everlasting life (cf. Gen. 2:9 and 3:22). Also, in the New Testament, a tree in the heavenly Jerusalem whose leaves are for healing the nations (cf. Rev. 22:2).

triad -- a union or set of three; a group of three persons, things ideas, etc.; a trinity: hence Holy Triad = Holy Trinity.

Ultimate Man, the -- a term coined by Bishop Nikolai to describe Jesus Christ as the Son of God, as the "new Adam," as the ideal, total, complete and Ultimate Man *(Svechovek),* who possesses the pure, true and genuine nature of unfallen man as well as the divine nature of God the Father in His divine-human personality. All who unite themselves to the God-man, Jesus Christ, regain the fullness of their "ultimate humanity," which the descendants of Adam have lost since the expulsion from the Garden of Eden.

Wisdom -- one of the appellations of Jesus Christ in the Bible. Cf. 1 Cor. *1:24*-- "Christ the power of God and the wisdom of God." Christian theol ogy also links Christ to certain passages about wisdom in the Old Testament (cf. Proverbs 9:1-11).

Word of God -- in Christian theology, the *Logos* or *Word;* Jesus Christ as the second person of the Holy Trinity.

yoga -- (Sanskrit = "union") in Hindu philosophy a practice involving intense and complete concentration upon something, especially the deity, in order to establish identity of consciousness with the object of concentration: it is a mystic and ascetic practice, usually involving the discipline of prescribed postures, controlled breathing, etc.

Zoroaster -- (c. 628 B.C. - c. 551 B.C.) religious teacher and prophet of ancient Persia who founded Zoroastrianism.

Zoroastrianism -- the religious system of the Persians before their conversion to Islam. Its principles include belief in an afterlife and in the continuous struggle of the universal spirit of good (Ormazd) with the spirit of evil (Ahriman), the good ultimately to prevail.

Translator's Notes to the Introduction

1. Cf. Acts 2:2-4 which relates how on the feast of Pentecost the Holy Spirit rushed down from heaven and tongues of fire appeared above the apostles' heads: "And they were all filled with the Holy Spirit and began to speak with other tongues, as the Spirit gave them utterance."
Also, the word *Vladika* translated here as "Master" is identical to the word translated as "Bishop" above.

2. "Rastko" was St. Sava's name as a youth in his father's palace, before he ran away to the monasteries of the holy mountain of Athos in his seventeenth year, at which time he was given his monastic name of "Sava."
The last part of this sentence is in Church Slavonic, *vsesozhenija za vsjeh i vsja,* and echoes wording found in the Divine Liturgy.

3. St. Simeon the New Theologian (949-1022) was the greatest of Byzantine mystical writers. In his teaching he assigned a central place to the vision of Divine Light, while being at the same time strongly Christocentric.

4. St. Macarius the Great was an Egyptian monk and priest (c. 300 -c. 390).

5. In place of "Bishop," the original Serbian *test* reads "Father" *(otac),* probably because this term of address appears in the *troparion* to his namesake, St. Nicholas the Wonderworker and Archbishop of Myra.

Made in the USA
Lexington, KY
04 May 2019